N.W. Gilbert

Willoughby's Wisdom

A story of New England country life in by-gone days

N.W. Gilbert

Willoughby's Wisdom

A story of New England country life in by-gone days

ISBN/EAN: 9783337427559

Printed in Europe, USA, Canada, Australia, Japan

Cover: Foto ©ninafisch / pixelio.de

More available books at **www.hansebooks.com**

Willoughby's Wisdom

A STORY

OF

NEW ENGLAND COUNTRY LIFE

IN BY-GONE DAYS

BY
N. W. GILBERT

BOSTON
PUBLISHED BY THE AUTHOR
1890

Copyright, 1890,
By N. W. GILBERT.
All rights reserved.

PREFACE.

LET no reader imagine that a new literary character has come upon the stage. The writing of a simple, short story, in prose or song — even though it should be conceded to have been written in respectable verse — by no means makes a man of letters. And this is strictly an amateur performance. One, it is true, into which I have put considerable effort, it having occupied a large part of the little leisure I have had for a number of years. And it has helped to while away many an otherwise sad and lonely hour. If it shall do as much for my readers, even in the aggregate, it will not have been written in vain.

My motives have been, to produce a readable story, that somebody might get interested in, and also to put on record some phases of social and religious life in rural New England a half century ago, which have since disappeared, or are now rapidly passing away.

My language is commonplace and familiar. I have made free use of the pronouns I and you, both as a matter of convenience and a matter of choice; as it seems to bring writer and reader somewhat nearer together, and so into closer sympathy with each other, provided the writing be such as shall tend to attract rather than to repel. And to whoever approaches the door of my little literary air castle, I say most cordially, Come in and sit down. Make yourself quite at home. We shall be all by ourselves, and we can talk about our neighbors as freely as we like. I will speak well of some of them; and even that is not always done. I may reveal some of their secrets, but they came to me without the customary promise not to tell. And that the narrations herein contained may prove sufficiently interesting and instructive to compensate all readers for their time and money, and that we may separate on more friendly terms than the commercial ones which have brought us together, is the earnest wish of

THE AUTHOR.

WILLOUGHBY'S WISDOM.

CANTO FIRST.

I.

'Twas many years ago, in early spring,
   And on a pleasant Sunday; I should say
About the last of April, as I bring
   Old recollections up, or first of May:
The buds were out, the birds were on the wing,
   Although the earth was still in sombre gray,
Dismantled of its white and snowy sheen,
And waiting for its robe of summer green.

II.

I say the earth, I mean that part of it,
   Wherein occurred, by fortune or by fate,
The commonplace events which, seeming fit
   For warp or woof of what I would relate,
I weave into my song; with how much wit,
   Or sense, I cannot say; and so must wait,
Until the public verdict, being had,
Proclaims it good, indifferent or bad.

III.

Midway between two little country towns,
   Along the base of that Green Mountain range,
Above whose lofty peaks old Mansfield frowns,
   And looks upon a scene of constant change,

On lake and river, hill and meadow downs,
  On many a peaceful home and quiet grange,
Where sways the graceful elm and towers the pine,
And where the bleating sheep and lowing kine

IV.

Roam o'er the verdant slopes to satiate
  An appetite that's keen for native food,
Then lie beneath the trees and ruminate,
  In seeming happy and contented mood,
Or patiently stand waiting by the gate,
  Or graze again some fresh and tempting rood —
Here long ago some incidents occurred,
Of which the world at large has never heard.

V.

Between these towns, and on the old highway,
  Which, night and morning, witnessed the approach
Of that famed monarch of a former day,
  The heavy laden, rapid running coach,
O'er which the driver held despotic sway —
  And on his rights 'twere dangerous to encroach,
For horse or man, at least for boys who tried
To hang upon the rack and run or ride.

VI.]

That old stage-coach, by nimble horses drawn,
  With its attendant clatter, dust and din,
Has served its purpose and, alas! is gone;
  And now the iron horse comes neighing in:
Some passengers get off, some more get on,
  The uniformed conductor may have been
The gallant driver, in the days of yore,
Of the pretentious stage-coach, now no more.

VII.

Well, on this old stage road there used to stand,
  Between the villages, as I have said,
Upon an elevated piece of land,
  A farmer's dwelling-house, with L and shed;
And from the intervale on either hand,
  A private carriage-way obliquely led
Thereto; commencing fifty yards or so,
From where the house looked on the road below.

VIII.

Two barns were also standing on the same
  Convenient rise, which nature had designed,
Apparently with philanthropic aim,
  Of thus conferring favors on mankind;
At least upon the one who should réclaim,
  From native solitude, the place we find
These buildings on, this higher spot of ground,
Which overlooked the intervale around.

IX.

The intervale was smooth, at least not rough,
  The elevation mentioned was not high,
Not quite what, in the west, they'd call a bluff,
  Or in the east a hill, against the sky.
Its altitude was moderate, just enough
  To be convenient, pleasant, sandy, dry;
And in Vermont at least, a house will stand
The test of wisdom, built upon the sand.

X.

Or sand and gravel, with a little loam,
  Which this contained, a good convenient soil
Whereon to found a hearthstone and a home,
  In which to rest from weariness of toil;

Where children may return who haply roam,
  To seek repose where filial love may coil
Around the parent hearts, which ever burn
With stronger love than children e'er return.

XI.

The house and L stood fronting to the east,
  A little south of which, the barns, in form
Of half a square, gave shelter to the beast,
  That sought protection from the wintry storm ;
Kept out the wind — to some extent at least —
  Let in the genial sunshine, bright and warm,
Which cows and sheep may love, as well as men,
Whene'er released from stable and from pen.

XII.

I said 'twas on a pleasant Sunday in
  The long ago, that certain things befell,
Which I must chronicle, and so begin
  The story which I had designed to tell.
'Tis not a pleasant thing to speak of sin,
  In close connection with the old church bell,
Which had successively been rung and tolled,
To call the worshippers into the fold.

XIII.

And yet the truth requires that I should say —
  At least if I should say it, 'twould be true —
That here, in one of these two barns, that day,
  We might have seen four daring youngsters, who
Were sitting in a circle on the hay,
  And by the modest light the cracks let through,
Between the boards, contracted at each edge,
Were playing at the game we call old sledge.

XIV.

They were but novices at such a game,
  They hadn't played extensively before,
A fact which I may hardly need to name,
  The oldest but thirteen, or little more;
'Twas not to be expected they could claim
  A large amount of this peculiar lore,
Whereby to judge correctly of the use
To which 'twere best to put the ace or deuce.

XV.

George Hayden was a lad just past thirteen,
  Whose father lived some half a mile away,
Directly to the southward from the scene
  Which I have just described upon the hay;
Have just commenced describing it, I mean —
  His nose was Roman and his eyes were gray,
His form symmetrical, though rather slight,
He wasn't scholarly, but keen and bright.

XVI.

His brother Willoughby was only ten;
  His birthday coming a few weeks before
The time of which I write; and even then,
  He showed some leanings to scholastic lore,
And frequently would listen to the men,
  As often they debated, o'er and o'er,
The long contested claims, respectively,
Of Federalism and Democracy.

XVII.

And Nathan Alden was between the two,
  In point of age, as reckoned by the date
Of birth — a stout and chubby fellow who,
  Although in intellect perhaps not great,

In muscular estate was well-to-do;
　　The other boys agreed, at any rate,
That he was hard to match in feats of strength,
At rough-and-tumble, side-hold or arms-length.

XVIII.

And he was fond of exercising this,
　　His chief accomplishment, on any one,
Among his fellows, who should go amiss
　　In moral conduct, or in having done
Some fancied wrong; and none attained the bliss
　　Of being able constantly to shun
Some trifling breach of his imperious and
Unwritten law, as shifting as the sand.

XIX.

In fact, the law was made to suit the case,
　　Directly after it had been transgressed;
And executed in as brief a space
　　As guilt were proven in, or even guessed;
A quite convenient method, in the face
　　Of all the facts, to settle what were best,
As fancy might suggest, or passion bid,
As many do — as then young Nathan did.

XX.

They called him Nate, to make a shorter name,
　　And I shall deem it not at all unfair,
And not disparaging to his good fame,
　　If I should chance to use it here and there;
Or Nate or Nathan it were all the same,
　　Like Ralph or Ralpho — Hudibras's Squire —
Which Butler said he should be free to call him,
Recording faithfully what might befall him.

XXI.

Tim Turner once, a sprightly little soul,
  Was on his way to school, and unattended
By George and Will, on whom, as cheek by jowl,
  Especially with Will, he much depended
For his protection to and from the goal
  He now was striving for; but unbefriended,
On this occasion, he went past the house
Where Deacon Alden lived, and his good spouse.

XXII.

He wasn't running, but he briskly walked,
  And hoped he might get by unseen by Nate,
Whose notions of humility were shocked,
  By his straightforward look and rapid gait,
As he observed him, and he swiftly stalked,
  Or rushed upon him at a furious rate,
And seized him by the coat, and " jest to show "
That he was " master," threw him in the snow.

XXIII.

But after that the two walked arm-in-arm,
  Until at length they reached the district school ;
And Tim, subdued, received no farther harm,
  Except by being called a " little fool,"
Which lent another luster to the charm
  Of education, and the wholesome rule
Of old-time pedagogues, whose valiant deeds
Supplied our discipline and mental needs.

XXIV.

O lust of power! which undermines apace,
  The righteousness of almost any ruler;
And powerfully checks the " growth in grace,"
  Of him who governs army, church or school or

Dominion, save in Prince Siddartha's case,
  (As chronicled by Arnold and Max Müller,)
And other few, but Buddha lacked the merit
Of righteous rule he did not yet inherit.

XXV.

O district school! and each imperious master,
  That lorded over it in days of yore!
How oft I wished the seasons would go faster,
  In early youth, and even mildly swore —
Although I'd met with no extreme disaster —
  That I would try and even up the score,
For what I had endured — with great humility —
Should I possess the muscular ability.

XXVI.

And time supplied me that, but I had learned
  That we must all eventually receive,
From nature's balance sheets, what we have earned;
  At least I've come sincerely to believe
We must, and that we need not be concerned
  For others' sins, so much as we should grieve
In memory of our own, which round us throng —
Or seek revenge for real or fancied wrong.

XXVII.

So I condemn my masters only through
  A higher power, as did the great Saint Paul
The wicked coppersmith, who sought to do
  The saint " much evil," when he just let fall
An earnest prayer — I think a just one too,
  Which we may safely use concerning all
Schoolmasters, whether Christians, Jews or Turks,
Whom Heaven " reward according to their works."

XXVIII.

But I digress, and I will now return,
  To where I left the party on the hay,
To give some facts from which the world might learn
  Just who they were ; but I forgot to say
Tim Turner was the fourth, and he would spurn
  A mild suggestion that he couldn't play
" As well's the rest " —wherein perhaps he might,
Although the youngest, have been nearly right;

XXIX.

For he had been allowed to play at home,
  A privilege the others hadn't had ;
They having been compelled to always roam,
  In search of pleasure, which is always bad
For children who, beneath the parent dome,
  Should all, at times, be " riotously glad,"
With sports and games intended to amuse them,
And thus be taught to moderately use them.

XXX.

But Mr. Hayden entertained a notion
  That children should be rather strictly reared ;
Suppressing every juvenile emotion,
  Excepting such as he himself revered ;
And so, with an unwavering devotion,
  He taught his own such precepts as appeared
To him commendable and wise and true,
Most strict in morals and in manners too,

XXXI.

He always paid the latter great attention,
  Enforcing them with a peculiar zest.
Propriety is not a late invention,
  And what of true politeness to a guest,

He didn't know, 'tis not worth while to mention,
   Or carry forward to the very best
Of his ability; and his ability
Was very great in matters of civility.

XXXII.

But I digress again, the common lot
   Of story tellers, as it seems to be;
Although the widow Hezekiah Bedott
   Assured the world with emphasis, that she
Believed in always coming straight to what
   She had designed to say; and as for me,
I'll tell what further happened on the hay,
Before the truant urchins got away.

XXXIII.

Though I perhaps should say, in common suavity,
   That Deacon Alden owned the fair estate
I've partially described; a man of gravity,
   Who gave to " worldly things " but little weight,
And who believed in the complete depravity
   Of all mankind; and thought it was innate;
A faith which then extended far and wide,
And still quite frequently seems verified.

XXXIV.

I said 'twas Sunday, but the village spire,
   Which pointed reverently towards the sky,
And beckoned to the world to " come up higher,"
   And to the faithful to be drawing nigh
To where upon the altar burned the fire,
   Whose brightness wasn't seen but by the eye
Of faith, was three or four long miles away,
From where my youthful heroes spent the day.

XXXV.

And there Nate's older brothers went to hear
  The joyful tidings of salvation free,
Their father had embraced for many a year,
  Instructing them therein in some degree,
Although to him it still seemed pretty clear
  They needed further teaching more than he,
So he remained at home, content to search
The sacred word, while sending them to church.

XXXVI.

Although there were, in that same neighborhood,
  Devout religious services that day;
Where any seeker after truth, who would,
  Might hear good Elder Sherman preach and pray;
A blacksmith and a minister, who could,
  By turns, drive horseshoe nails and drive away
The enemy of souls; and plainly tell
The road to heaven — the other road as well.

XXXVII.

'Twas at the schoolhouse, half a mile or so,
  From where the Aldens lived, and towards the town;
Where my young friends were given leave to go,
  And listen to the truth as there laid down,
By those deemed competent at least to show,
  On what conditions to avoid the frown
Of God's displeasure, and securely hold
A safe position in the Christian fold.

XXXVIII.

Nate started off, but seeing George and Will
  Were coming up the road, with little Tim,
He walked in their direction slowly, till
  The parties met, when George accosted him,

"How are you Nate? you look dressed up to kill;" —
   His clothes were tidy and he did look trim —
"Did anybody know when you got back,
The other night, from playing high-low-jack?"

XXXIX.

Which, thus referring to a former game,
   Suggested also that it would be quite
Enjoyable again to do the same,
   And one remarked that "like enough" they might;
And all to that conclusion quickly came,
   Provided they were safely out of sight;
As presently they were, as we have seen,
The barn walls making a sufficient screen.

XL.

They found a clean half-bushel standing in
   The granary, wherein was kept in store,
In subdivisions of the ample bin,
   Oats, corn and wheat, of which there still was more
Or less remaining. "This is neat's a pin,"
   Said George, inverting it upon the floor,
For on the mow he thought they would be able
To make of it a quite convenient table.

XLI.

They had no seats, but sat upon the hay,
   In primitive position round the measure;
And thus, in quite an unpretentious way,
   Commenced what they regarded as a pleasure;
Instead of the improvement of the day,
   In laying up some little store of treasure,
In that bright haven of man's future weal,
Where moth will not corrupt and thieves not steal.

XLII.

"I'll save my ace," said Nathan, as he drew
    From out his hand, and on the other three,
Already played, and nearly worthless, threw
    The ace of trumps; which you and I can see
Was less sagacious — though the best he knew,
    From what he'd seen of playing then — than he
Himself regarded it; a grand mistake,
Which inexperience must often make.

XLIII.

"The ace," observed his partner, who was Will,
    "Don't need no savin', for it takes 'em all;
And when you have it you should keep it till
    You have a chance to swing;" which seemed to call
In question his ability, or skill,
    And intimate that it was rather small;
Which, though 'twas true, and though 'twas kindly meant,
Appeared to him somewhat impertinent.

XLIV.

And he replied quite earnestly, "I know
    As much, I guess, about this game, as you;
I've seen the big boys play, and they play so —
    And seen 'em play it 'fore you ever knew
Enough to tell which card was high or low;"
    And thus enforcing what he deemed was due,
In deference to seniors, Nate removed
The trick, for taking which, he'd been reproved.

XLV.

It being now his turn to play again —
    Will being notified to keep his place —
He came to partly comprehend that when
    A player held the king or queen or ace,

It might be well to "swing" for jack or ten,
    Especially the former, which, in case
It should be captured, counted him the same
    As high or low, or one point in the game.

XLVI.

He thought it over, but as he could bring
    Himself to no decision, condescended
To say inquiringly, "Now I can swing,"
    As if it were the course he had intended;
For his remaining hand contained the king,
    Which he would play if it were recommended;
And hesitatingly he looked at Will,
Half throwing down the card, but holding still.

XLVII.

"No talking crossboard," here demanded Tim,
    For he, as luck would have it, held the jack,
Which was the only trump dealt off to him,
    Of all the baker's dozen in the pack,
Which made the prospect seem a little grim,
    If his opponent swung, which now, alack!
Was threatened, and he knew it was but fair,
That all the rules should be observed with care.

XLVIII.

"You mind your business: I shall say and do,"
    Retorted Nate, "jest what I please about
What I shall lead with, and I'll lick you too,
    You little fool you, if you don't look out;"
A threat he'd willingly have carried through,
    Had circumstances favored it, no doubt,
But as it was, some future time must bide,
While Tim in bristling eloquence replied,

XLIX.

" No you won't lick me nuther," and his eye
    Was flashing with defiance all the while,
" You can't do no such thing, you das'n't try,
    You great, stout lummox, you, you dasn't, I'll —"
Here his bravado was determined by
A sound which, grating harshly, like a file,
On all their ears, at once was recognized,
And they were no less frightened than surprised.

L.

'Twas made by turning round the old halfmoon,
    Or crescent fastener which held the door,
That opened from the yard; and very soon
    A well-known step was heard upon the floor ;
And as the dial was approaching noon,
    They knew that one or two short minutes more,
And Deacon Alden would be on the mow,
Where they were busy with their playing now.

LI.

They were expecting him, but thought he would
    Have been a half hour later at the least ;
And being well aware the buildings stood
    In such position he must pass the east,
And enter from the southern side, they should,
    They thought, detect the sound long ere it ceased,
Of his approaching footsteps, when they might
Get on the " high beams," safely out of sight.

LII.

And this they would have done, I have no doubt,
    At any point of time except the one
Wherein unhappily it came about,
    The little angry scrimmage was begun ;

And which, the very moment he came out,
   Was at its height; and ere the fray was done —
Save by the creaking of the great barn door —
He unannounced, stepped in upon the floor.

LIII.

They saw the situation at a glance —
   A mental glance, which came to them by sound;
Wherein was nothing seen but sore mischance,
   In view of which, in silence most profound,
They stood in fear — which ever doth enhance
   Our present woes — and scarce could look around.
Tim's courage was all gone, and Nathan's too,
The latter whispering, "What shall we do?"

LIV.

He said no more, and could have made no move,
   To further any plan of extrication,
From what appeared, and what would doubtless prove,
   To be a rather awkward situation.
Will's thoughts ran slowly in the mental groove —
   He couldn't act without some meditation,
Requiring time; and 'twas too grave a case
For little Tim to meet with, face to face.

LV.

'Tis said that when a people are oppressed,
   By home misgovernment or foreign nation,
Until their grievances must be redressed,
   And when, to push some vital reformation,
They need a leader of a magic crest,
   Whose genius seems to come of inspiration,
The leader always comes; which reverential
And wise men have believed is Providential.

LVI.

I say not this is so, nor do I say
   That it is not; but rather, by evasion,
I leave the reader free to have his way,
   In his beliefs, without undue persuasion;
But this I say — as frequently we may —
   That there was one who equalled the occasion
We're now considering, and made amends
For lack of effort by his younger friends.

LVII.

George Hayden I have said was but a lad,
   And he could not endure a mental strain,
Perhaps, beyond his years; and yet he had
   A nimble finger and a nimble brain;
And to his other merits we may add
   That (which, if old or young, but few maintain,
With judgment such as needs but slight revision,)
Of quick perception and of prompt decision.

LVIII.

In other words, he could decide instanter,
   In many cases, what 'twere best to do;
He reasoned in a sort of moral canter,
   On great occasions, like the one in view,
Where ordinary wits would balk and banter,
   Until the opportunity fell through;
As I have squandered many an opportunity,
Because my mental powers were not in unity.

LIX.

He hesitated but an instant, when
   He had discovered, or devised a way
By which they might escape detection; then
   He whispered, "Quick, get underneath the hay:"

And ne'er was warrior, marshalling his men,
  Obeyed with more alacrity than they
Displayed in executing his commands,
By quick and dexterous use of feet and hands.

LX.

The shrinkage of the mow made some beginning,
  Or helped to much more readily begin
The game they had but little chance of winning,
  Which they, however, were in hopes to win;
And at the terminus of their "first inning —"
To use a sporting phrase — they all were in
Between the boards and hay; a situation
That screened them partially from observation.

LXI.

But one important thing they all forgot,
  Which threatened to assume an ugly shape;
And 'twas a question if they now were not
  In what might prove a still more serious scrape;
For this new difficulty seemed full fraught
  With danger — which they yet might not escape —
Of placing him they fled from face to face
With all the facts pertaining to the case.

LXII.

They'd left the pack of cards where they were laid,
  Upon the measure, when the trump was turned;
Except the ones they held, and hadn't played,
  Which they had quite instinctively inurned
In their side pockets, ere their flight was made;
  And when George thought of this, which now concerned
So unmistakably, their future weal,
He feared it might the whole affair reveal.

LXIII.

And even then, from out his hiding-place,
  He thrust his head, and glanced around anew,
To see if he might cautiously retrace
  His one misstep; but coming into view,
He saw the old slouched hat and solemn face
  Of Deacon Alden, and again withdrew,
To wait, as needs he must, to see what next;
Chagrined, defeated, puzzled and perplexed.

LXIV.

And now the deacon stepped upon the mow,
  And chanced to turn his eyes directly where
The measure stood; and then with knitted brow,
  He murmured to himself, "I do declare!
What have those reckless boys been up to now?
  And why should they have left their things right there,
Especially the cards? which they are sure
To always put where they will be secure."

LXV.

He slowly turned to where his pitchfork lay,
  "They can't be up here now?" he queried, as
He looked upon the beams, and in the bay,
  And all about, "no, I am sure there has
Been no one here; besides, they went away
  To church. It must have been, and doubtless was,
Last night, for I remember mother said
She heard them going up quite late to bed."

LXVI.

And he resolved to sacrifice the pack,
  Or what was left of it, and place it where
It could entice no more to ruin's track,
  Its youthful owners, in its evil snare;

At least he'd see that when they should come back
    To look for it, they shouldn't find it there;
And thus while vindicating heaven's law,
He busily threw down his hay and straw.

LXVII.

Young George, meanwhile, had not been idle in
    His hiding-place, but slyly peering through
His rustic covering, so loose and thin,
    Had been determining what he could do;
If it were possible he yet might win,
    And save, perchance, his reputation too;
For he himself regarded getting under
The hay without the cards, a sort of blunder.

LXVIII.

He saw the deacon once or twice, who seemed
    Quite busy with the hay he chanced to get
Some distance from the cards, and so he deemed
    It likely that he hadn't seen them yet;
A kindly circumstance, through which there gleamed
    A lingering hope; in view of which he set
Himself to work to cautiously fulfill
A purpose which he hoped might serve them still.

LXIX.

He wasn't more than half a dozen feet
    From where the measure stood; and it occurred
To him that he perhaps might yet compete
    Successfully — and not be seen or heard —
For what were now a prize; and thus complete
    The safety of their flight. He gently stirred,
And pushed the yielding hay to right and left,
And crawled along the seam he thus had cleft,

LXX.

Until he reached a point from which he thrust
  His hand up through the hay, beside the measure,
And with commendable, undoubting trust,
  In Providence or fortune, had the pleasure
(As commonly such great persistence must)
  Of grasping in his hand the longed-for treasure;
Which he withdrew, but he was still in fear
The deacon might have chanced to see or hear,

LXXI.

His *coup d'état;* and anxiously he lay,
  And listened for the sound, his ears to thrill,
Of further rustling of the deacon's hay,
  Which he had heard so constantly until
The present; but the sound had died away,
  And now no longer reached him. All was still;
Unless we should, perhaps, except the beating
Which his own heart was rapidly repeating.

LXXII.

The stillness was, however, broken when,
  A moment afterwards, he heard the tread
Of footsteps going down the ladder, then
  Across the floor, and rapidly they sped:
The great door on its hinges swung again,
  The deacon had precipitately fled;
As was apparent to the listening ear,
Until the sound it could no longer hear.

LXXIII.

No sooner had George listened to the last
  Faint, lingering echo of the footsteps' fall,
Than (as a feudal chieftain's bugle blast
  Might bring his followers to moat and wall),

Emerging from the hay, and having cast
  A hasty glance around, his muffled call
Of "boys, he's gone," brought face to face with him,
His waiting fellows, Nathan, Will and Tim.

LXXIV.

Said Tim, "Did he git all the cards there, say?"
  "I reckon not," said George, "but he'll git us,
Unless we hurry up and git away
  From here darned soon" — the mild and only "cuss
Word" often used by him — "he didn't stay
  To do his fodderin'; there'll be a muss
When he comes back, I'll bet, unless we're gone,"
Then saying in commanding tones, "come on,"

LXXV.

He led the way to where the ladder stood,
  Descending which, he walked across the floor,
As quickly as conveniently he could,
  And very cautiously unclasped the door,
For he conjectured that the deacon would
  Be likely to return, perhaps before
They would be able to get safely hence,
Across the yard and o'er the lofty fence.

LXXVI.

But this they soon accomplished, when they were,
  At least for now, well out of danger's reach,
Debating as to what might yet occur,
  —Indulging in congratulative speech;
And thanking all the saints the calendar
  Enumerates, or catechisms teach,
That they had thus escaped what might have been
A bad predicament to have been in.

LXXVII.

It only now remained for Nate to get
  Into the house; and he, perchance, would learn
That such an undertaking was beset
  With dangers which might justly give concern;
Although it must not be attempted yet,
  Until the time arrived for his return
From morning service at the schoolhouse, where
  They hadn't reached as yet the closing prayer.

LXXVIII.

George thought it over hastily and said,
  " You go along behind the buildings till
You git the other side, and in the shed,
  And hide behind the woodpile and keep still;
Or git up on the timbers overhead,
  And when you hear 'em comin', as you will
'Fore long, from meet'n, then as still's a mouse,
Slip out the shed and go right in the house."

LXXIX.

Which he, according to his orders, did ;
  Or rather, which he undertook to do,
As nearly as he could as he was bid;
  While George and Will and Tim ran quickly to
The little brook a few rods off and hid,
  Behind some bushes which they might look through ;
The " beaver meadow brook," 'twas called, which crossed
The road, and running eastward, soon was lost

LXXX.

In Joe's brook, or " the great brook," which its way
  From thence pursued to river, lake and sea ;
And here the truants had designed to stay,
  In safe concealment, till it seemed to be

Judicious to go home ; where they would say
   But little of the meeting, or agree
'Twas " 'bout as common," if interrogated,
Wherein the truth should not be overstated,

LXXXI.

To any great extent, they rightly thought,
   Although we must admit they would thereby,
Have done what Jerry Train, the drover, sought,
   By sheer deception, deep and dark and sly,
To do, when he from purest fiction, wrought
" A truth which artfully concealed a lie ;"
As many a lie has often been concealed,
By truth which was but partially revealed.

LXXXII.

" I wonder," queried George. "if Nate got in
   The woodshed, as I told him to, and what
He's up to now. If he plays so's to win,
   And gits into the house and don't git caught,
We're all right, and they won't know where we've been."
   " Hum ! " muttered Tim, " they'll ketch him, like as not,
I'll bet if I was there I'd keep away —
But didn't I stump him pretty smart though, say ? "

LXXXIII.

" Yes," George replied, "you stumped him smart enough,
   But then you wouldn't if you hadn't known
That Will and I was there. You wouldn't bluff
   Him that way much if you should be alone
With him, for you'd git handled mighty rough,
   As once last winter, when you had to own
You dasn't go to school alone ; and one
Time when you met him, that you cut and run."

LXXXIV.

"I guess you'd run," said he, in more subdued,
 And milder tones, "if you'd been where I was,
That day last winter, cold as 'twas, and you'd
 Been ducked and had your face washed, all because
You wouldn't own you'd sassed him "— some old feud
 Referring to, that hinged on private laws,
And arbitrary rule, — " I'll bet you'd do
Jest what I did; you're older 'n he is, too."

LXXXV.

While thus his prowess and his grievances,
 He dwelt upon by turns, young Nate, instead,
Was quite successfully performing his
 Allotted task. He got into the shed,
Unseen by mortal; which should be, and is,
 Recorded to his credit; as 'tis said
The only rule the world will even profess
To judge us by, is failure or success.

LXXXVI.

And thus far he succeeded very well,
 But climbing up upon the wood pile, he,
By awkwardness or chance — I cannot tell
 Exactly which, I wasn't there to see —
Displaced it slightly, whereupon it fell,
 And with a crash quite loud enough to be
Distinctly heard some little distance round,
The wood and he came tumbling to the ground.

LXXXVII.

That he was frightened, we may safely say,
 If ordinary methods may be trusted,
Of ascertaining facts, and there he lay,
 Considering himself completely "busted;"

Although he would have tried to get away,
   Or as the modern phrase is, would have " dusted,"
But there was no convenient place to dust;
And so he did what such an urchin must,

LXXXVIII.

In such predicament; he quickly got
   Upon his feet, and looking towards the door,
He stood and trembled, as of course he thought
   The time of his prosperity was o'er;
That they would presently be out, and what
   The dickens he should do or say, was more
Than he could tell; but as they didn't come,
He thanked his stars, although his lips were dumb.

LXXXIX.

Moreover, he proceeded to express
   His gratitude for being let alone,
When he had stood a minute, more or less,
   Until his wits had come to be his own,
Or he had come to normally possess
   The faculties so lately overthrown —
By getting into two old empty barrels,
In hopes to " save his bacon " and his laurels.

XC.

I say two barrels, he got into one,
   Which proved too small to hold him at his ease,
And turned another over it, which done,
   He stood erect and hidden; and in these,
Although 'tis true some little risk was run,
   He felt as snug as old Diogenes,
When living in his tub; and all unknown,
And undisturbed, he there remained alone,

XCI.

For half an hour or so, until he heard
  The wagons coming slowly down the road,
And people talking; and it then occurred
  To him he'd best be changing his abode;
And slipping through the door — not having erred
  In point of time — as in his breast there glowed
The rapture of success, which he had earned —
He walked into the house quite unconcerned.

XCII.

Now Nathan had a pious old grandmother;
  And what benighted one of us has not —
Or hasn't had, at least, sometime or other,
  Though now she may be gone and quite forgot?
And grandmas " stick much closer than a brother,"
  Insisting their descendants shall be taught
The good old way, and made to walk therein,
To shun the paths of evil and of sin.

XCIII.

His father's mother — and she lived with them,
  In patient waiting for the great " I Am,"
To crown her with the Christian's diadem,
  To call her to himself and to the Lamb.
As much more righteous than the world, as Shem
  And Japheth were than was their brother Ham,
She waited, as I say, for the reward
Of those who most devoutly " love the Lord."

XCIV.

She loved this grandchild too, perhaps no less,
  Though not in such a reverential way;
She loved his person, and she sought to bless
  His soul, for which she ne'er forgot to pray:

And while she met him with a fond caress,
  On this occasion, she went on to say —
When she had called him to her side, and thrown
  Her arms around him — in a solemn tone,

XCV.

"You know, my child, how often you've been warned
  Against the wicked practices of men
And boys who play at cards." Had she suborned,
  Or summoned witnesses to prove that then
He'd just been playing, and if he had scorned,
  Like Washington, to tell a whopper when
It would have served him, he could not have been
More startled and surprised. The tears came in

XCVI.

His eyes, for when the cards were mentioned, he
  Suspected that somehow the truth was out:
His father sat close by, and seemed to be
  In meditation, or perhaps in doubt;
His mother too was near, and seeing she
  Was looking earnestly, he was about
Half ready to confess the whole affair,
And take the consequences then and there.

XCVII.

But grandma kindly said, "Don't cry, my dear,
  For I'm not going to chide you, only tell
What happened in the barn." Poor Nathan here
  Grew pale again, and from his cheek there fell,
Upon her wrinkled hand, an honest tear;
  For he was frightened — puzzled too, as well,
To catch the hidden meaning of it all,
While tears continued rapidly to fall.

XCVIII.

"Don't cry," continued she, "for you have been
  To meeting, like a good, well-meaning lad ;
I hope the preacher pointed out the sin
  Of playing cards, so dangerous and bad —
But don't you think the boys were playing in
  The barn last night?" By this time Nathan had
Begun to see the turn that things were taking,
And so left off his crying and his quaking.

XCIX.

"At least," she presently went on to say,
  " The reasons why we think so, seem so good,
We have but little doubt; for when, to day,
  Your father went to give the cows their food,
And got upon the mow, there on the hay,
  His own half-bushel, bottom upwards, stood,
And on it lay a pack of cards, as when
They had been played, or might be played again.

C.

"The 'ten of hearts,' whatever that may be,
  Had been ' turned up for trump,' your father said —
A card with spots, as he explained to me,
  In shape like human hearts, and colored red ;
A thing I wish that you might never see,
  By which so many human souls are led
Away from Him who died to save mankind,
And from the 'narrow path' which 'few shall find.'

CI.

" But what I've told you now, my child, is not
  The strangest part of what I had to tell ;
At least it isn't what your father thought
  Most unaccountable of what befell;

Though I have long believed, and sometimes sought
  To prove to others that it is a well
Established fact that Satan always guards,
With jealous care, the players and the cards.

CII.

" And now it has been shown to be a fact,
  Beyond a doubt, or pretty nearly so;
The Evil one has been so plainly tracked,
  In what has just occurred, I almost know
(Although he wasn't noticed in the act,
  As he invisibly may come and go)
'Twas he himself; for there could be no one
But him to do what surely has been done.

CIII.

" For when your father got upon the mow,
  Where all was still, there being no one there,
He saw the cards, as I remarked just now,
  In plain sight lying on the measure, where
They doubtless had been used; and then, somehow,
  By unseen hand, or spirit of the air,
They disappeared; and when he looked again,
The cards were gone, and out of human ken."

CIV.

" And was the measure gone?" asked Nate, who seemed
  Less shocked than she apparently expected,
By revelations she so dreadful deemed,
  That all his hair might well have been erected;
As would her own, perhaps, if she had dreamed
  Of all the means by which he had detected
The error into which she had been led,
And error long by superstition fed.

CV.

" No, no, my child, the measure wasn't gone,"
    Grandma replied, " but 'tis enough to know,
That he took care of what was lying on
    The measure, or enough at least, to show
That he had come, and suddenly withdrawn;
    And some connection of the world below,
With wicked games; and cards especially,
Which lead to ruin, as I plainly see.

CVI.

" But that's not all; for when your father came
    Into the house and told us what the boys
Had done, and how that he of evil fame,
    Had used the arts which he alone employs,
I think that he was followed by the same
    Intruding spirit; for we heard a noise,
Out in the shed, as if a tier of wood
Had fallen to the ground; and why it should,

CVII.

" We couldn't see, as there was no one there,
    Unless it was the evil genius, who
Had come again, his presence to declare,
    To see if there was mischief yet to do;
And as we didn't any of us care
    To venture out to see if it was true
That any wood fell down when rumbling so,
We're still uncertain if it did or no."

CVIII.

" I'll go and see," said Nate, " I ain't afraid,"
    And suddenly he started towards the door,
And though she was surprised, and though she made
    Some strong objections, in a moment more,

The door was opened and the matter laid
  Before them, with the evidence which bore
Upon the case, whereon some light was thrown,
  And that the wood was down was clearly shown.

CIX.

"Why Nathan," Grandma said, "how dare you go
  Out there? Is it because you didn't hear
The crash, at which we all were startled so,
  Or is it that the good have naught to fear?"
Yet she herself was good, but didn't know
  What I do — and to me it seems quite clear
That, while our virtues may our fears dispel,
'Tis sometimes done by knowledge quite as well.

CX.

And Nate had some good reasons to believe
  That Grandma's theory was incorrect;
And, though he wasn't rapid to perceive
  A subtle truth, could easily detect
The error here. However she might weave
  Her superstitions round it, and connect
The warp and woof of Satan and of sin,
The "broken threads" could not be "woven in."

CXI.

Well, when the older boys got home from church,
  The deacon took them solemnly to do,
In such a way at first, as seemed to smirch
  The goodly record they referred him to;
But, though he prosecuted his research
  As best he might, could not discover who
It was that left the measure on the hay,
Wherefrom the cards were spirited away.

CXII.

For they, of course, could honestly deny
  All knowledge of the facts; they could, in sooth,
Have proven for themselves, an *alibi*,
  But that would have revealed an ugly truth,
More dangerous than a suspected lie;
  As many truths confront us in our youth,
That 'tis a little hard to frankly own,
And would be troublesome if they were known.

CXIII.

Their history was, in fact, somewhat akin,
  That evening, to the one that I've related
Of these, the smaller boys; for they were in
  The smithy, similarly situated;
The shop of Elder Sherman, which had been
  A place where boys had sometimes congregated,
To play at this old game of high-low-jack,
Though 'twas, of course, behind the elder's back;

CXIV.

Or in his absence, for he had a son,
  Who, though strong influence had been exerted
Thereto since early childhood was begun,
  Despite his preaching, wasn't yet converted;
And when the labors of the day were done,
  As by a plan that had been preconcerted,
With other boys he sometimes, in the shop,
Played games long after it was time to stop.

CXV.

But this the deacon didn't ascertain,
  And, though he questioned them concerning where
They were the night before, he didn't gain
  Much knowledge throwing light on this affair,

But counselled them in future to abstain
  From practices which might their souls ensnare,
And, partially recovered from the shock,
Which he'd received, went back to feed his stock.

CXVI.

Meanwhile the other boys, Tim, George and Will,
  Had left their hiding-place among the trees
And bushes, where they had remained until
  The " meetin' folks " appeared, when, seeing these,
George bade the others to " keep mighty still "
  About where they had been; then quite at ease,
They slowly walked along among the rest,
As each concealed the knowledge he possessed.

CXVII.

On reaching home, Will's mother asked if he
  Remembered anything the preacher said,
When George, conjecturing that he might be
  Unequal to the task, replied instead:
" He said " (and that was probable) " that we
  Must not play cards or dance, or else old Ned
Would git us, but I don't believe he knew,
For I can't see what hurt 'twill do, can you? "

CXVIII.

This served the purpose which he had designed,
  And called attention from the question to
The answer he had made; wherein we find
  A proposition, whether false or true,
That each may settle as he has a mind,
  Or has capacity for seeing through
A moral problem, and without confusion,
For coming to a rational conclusion.

CXIX.

Some earnest counsel then the mother gave,
  Concerning moral and divine affairs,
And virtues which she deemed most sure to save,
  And when she had resumed some household cares,
Will went for what his stomach seemed to crave,
  Into the pantry, and George went up stairs,
And with the hand his mother's lips had kissed,
Drew forth the cards and locked them in his " chist."

CXX.

And by the way, that " chist " of his was what
  I might denominate an institution ;
To which his earthly treasures he had brought,
  As on the world he levied contribution :
A varied list, the length of which was not
  Allowed to suffer any diminution,
For what he had acquired, when once 'twas there,
He watched and guarded with a miser's care.

CXXI.

Just what he had therein I cannot say,
  That is, I cannot give the list complete ;
Although I've seen and handled in my day,
  A few things which he used to there secrete.
He had a more or less obliging way,
  Though he was apt to make his favors meet
Some obligation which from him was due,
Or due him, being cancelled, to renew.

CXXII.

He had a book entitled " Abalino,"
  A quaint old story of an eastern swain —
Although concerning it but little I know —
  And used to loan it to his sister Jane,

For a consideration, not of rhino,
　　Like circulating libraries, for gain,
But something she could either say or do ;
　　And in the same way Will would get it too.

CXXIII.

But they could have it only by the hour,
　　And sometimes only half an hour a day;
Which made them feel at times a little sour,
　　And even angry; but it was the way
In which he would perpetuate his power,
　　Dominion, influence, control or sway;
As kings and emperors perpetuate
Their own, in managing affairs of state.

CXXIV.

He had some other domineering ways,
　　Exhibiting assumed superiority,
Which he was fond of in the early days
　　And years that long preceded his majority,
Exacting homage which submission pays
　　To those who, for the time, are in authority,
Which often is usurped, but holden still,
In bold defiance of its subjects' will.

CXXV.

O tyranny! thou hast as many forms,
　　As shapeless things in a kaleidoscope ;
And livest on the woes which come in swarms,
　　To drive away the sweet, delusive hope,
That men had cherished ; and which cheers and warms
　　Us ever as we onward blindly grope —
Base tyranny, which dost forever frown —
Of priest and king, of mitre and of crown.

CXXVI.

And thou, the tyranny of older boys!
How much the world has suffered from thy power;
How often hast thou filched away the joys
That natively belong to childhood's hour,
Till nature has restored the equipoise
Of justice and of right; and made thee cower
Before the subjects of thy late oppression,
Whose rights at length were in their own possession.

CXXVII.

Another interesting book George had,
The story of "Alonzo and Melissa";
The heroine and hero, he a lad
Who often quarrelled with the pretty miss he
Was making love to, which is always bad,
For lovers or for married people. This he,
However, remedied by magic power—
By living in a peace enchanted bower.

CXXVIII.

I wish somebody would invent a thing—
Or rather would construct a new condition
Of things which should, by love's enchantment, bring
A universal peace; that some magician
Might over human hearts a halo fling,
To justify the ancient premonition,
That peaceful men should make, in future years,
Plowshares and pruning hooks from swords and spears.

CXXIX.

That night, that is, the night succeeding to
The day on which occurred what I've related,
At ten o'clock or so, the actors who
Had played their several parts therein, as stated,

Had all begun successfully to woo
  The drowsy god, save two who, animated
By thoughts more serious, were wakeful still:
Grandma was one of these, the other Will.

CXXX.

The former was so thoroughly intent
  On making out the case she had begun,
In her own mind, according to its bent,
  And her conceptions of the "Evil One,"
To whom such superhuman power was lent,
  In all things happening beneath the sun,
That she her watchful vigils still was keeping,
Long after common mortals had been sleeping.

CXXXI.

The latter wasn't seeking to sustain
  The fact of diabolic interference,
By which old Clovenfoot attempts to gain
  Accessions to the host of his adherents,
But he was trying rather to explain
  A moral problem on its first appearance;
And in a way by which to be acquitted
Of wrongs which he already had admitted,

CXXXII.

As to himself, who, in a childish way,
  Was sitting now in judgment on the case;
As we must do when in the "judgment day,"
  Our own misdeeds confront us face to face;
And " we ourselves " shall be compelled to say
  We have not won as yet the moral race,
And " to the teeth and forehead of our faults,
To give in evidence " where virtue halts.

CXXXIII.

He then believed it was a deadly sin
  To play at cards, for so he had been taught;
A habit he had not been largely in,
  And one wherein he hadn't yet been caught,
By father or by mother, who had been
  So careful to instruct him as they ought,
In all which might secure his future weal,
And bring him to his manhood clean and leal.

CXXXIV.

And now besides the ordinary one
  Of doing that which he had been forbid,
He knew that he some other wrongs had done,
  Which might or might not easily be hid;
Which, independent of the hazard run,
  His own reproving conscience sorely chid;
He had deceived his mother, whose kind care
And love had sent him to the house of prayer.

CXXXV.

Besides, it was the holy sabbath day,
  That he had thus been led to desecrate,
In such unchristian, irreligious way
  As heaven's law might justly compensate,
By retribution which they tell us may,
  And often does, the guilty soul await,
Unless sincere repentance should forestall
The consequences of the ancient fall.

CXXXVI.

But he repented, and he even wept,
  In view of wrongs, too many far for one day,
And made a resolution ere he slept,
  That he would never play again on Sunday;

And he determined that it should be kept,
  Though not in deference to Mrs. Grundy,
Of whom he hadn't heard, but in compliance.
With what his mother taught as moral science.

CXXXVII.

And having thus repented of his sins —
  A shift to which sad mortals oft are driven,
In this frail world, whose moral outs and ins
  Require that souls should frequently be shriven,
When retribution for the past begins —
  And deeming he was partially forgiven,
And having earnestly essayed to pray,
He soundly slept the silent hours away.

WILLOUGHBY'S WISDOM.

CANTO SECOND.

I.

A Mr. Rollins lived half way between
   The deacon's house and Mr. Hayden's place,
Who had a boy, perhaps about eighteen,
   Or nineteen, as I recollect the face
His growing beard had just begun to screen;
   His form was tall, but had but little grace,
His character, I grieve to say, had less;
At least he wasn't famed for righteousness.

II.

A caustic writer says that every man
   Has faults enough to spoil him; and 'tis true
That every one has faults, as doubtless can
   Be demonstrated, as by me or you;
But when he puts all mortals under ban,
   To such extent of worthlessness, 'tis due
To God and man, to say it cannot be,
Since He created wisely you and me.

III.

But this Alfonso, whom they nicknamed Fon,
   Was quite as valueless, I think, as any
Whose character I ever studied on,
   If I can judge correctly by the many

Bad things I knew of him in days agone,
    Although he may perhaps receive his penny,
For service rendered, the eleventh hour,
To humankind, or to a higher power.

IV.

But when I knew him he was not a saint —
    Was rather quite an unregenerate sinner;
I think not from hereditary taint,
    His mother had much native goodness in her,
His father too, was fairly in restraint
    Of virtues which in him were vastly thinner
Than in the parent stock on either side;
Alas! that such sad things should e'er betide.

V.

Among the early pastimes which he had,
    Was to entice away a smaller boy,
(And I remember when I was a lad,
    To thus have fallen into his decoy;
Indeed a memory would be rather bad
    That failed to recollect it) and annoy
The helpless victim in all sorts of ways,
To make unhappy " happy childhood's days."

VI.

So too, young Willoughby, in early years,
    Well knew the force of his malicious bent,
And often struggled to keep back the tears,
    Within the lachrymals securely pent,
And suffered more or less from constant fears,
    Among the evils which the fates had sent,
Through this young lover of oppression, when
Beyond the reach of the parental ken.

VII.

Not evils such as would be quite unbearable,
　As I, perhaps, should say in Rollins' favor;
But saying much, it would be deemed but parable,
　By those who knew him when he was a shaver;
All moral garments were for him unwearable,
　All moral precepts were but " clishmaclaver,"
As Scotchmen say in their quaint Highland phrase –
At least not suited to his early days.

VIII.

But trials such as this, for instance; when
　Perchance they were alone upon the heather,
He'd seize Will's hands and hold them firmly, then
　Would rub or strike them rapidly together;
With moderate force, but o'er and o'er again,
　As millstones whirl, the upper o'er the nether,
Until between the friction and concussion,
He had been punished like a guilty Russian.

IX.

He didn't do it in an angry way,
　But in a seemingly good-natured one,
Pretending that in fact, 'twas only play —
　That all he wanted was "a little fun;"
Then cautioning his victim not to say
　A word concerning what had thus been done,
He'd smile upon him, knowing how to " smile
And smile, and be a villain " all the while.

X.

His father owned a farm of meadow land,
　Plateau and hill in requisite variety,
His brother Jack was three years older, and
　Had hoed potatoes, to his own satiety,

Until of age, when, hoping to command
    Respect and cash, and get in good society,
He went to town and with a merchant there,
Was selling dry goods, tin and wooden ware.

XI.

The father was a man of heavy frame,
    And being rather corpulent besides,
In easy circumstances too, he came
    At length to love his ease, and daily rides;
But turned an honest penny still the same,
    By buying butter, cheese, wool, beef and hides;
And other things, whose subsequent inflation
Of price, gave profit to the speculation.

XII.

This gave Alfonso largely the control
    Of things about the farm; and had he not
Been indolent, besides his lack of soul,
    It would have rendered worse the luckless lot
Of beast and boy, whose happiness he stole,
    Or cast a shadow over what they got,
By curse and whip, used freely at his work,
Which he, however, always tried to shirk.

XIII.

He had occasion once to go "to mill,"
    And though 'twas summer, or in early June,
The day was cold and raw; the air was chill,
    At even the meridian, or noon;
And having no one else, he offered Will
    A chance to ride; which seemed so opportune,
As such things do to boys, he didn't care
If he accepted; so they rode to where

XIV.

The old grist-mill had stood for many a day;
  'Twas not the one where "Little Jerry" ground,
Although its wood was wasting with decay,
  Its stones were crumbling and the wheels went round
With clattering noise, and dripping with the spray,
  And this, like that, "beneath the hill" was found,
But here the miller was of stalwart frame,
Although I fail to recollect his name.

XV.

Fon drove into the yard and, getting out,
  He gave the reins to Will and took the grist —
He piqued himself on being pretty stout,
  And deemed that strength of muscle was the gist
Of youthful virtues; and it was about
  The only one he had, I must insist;
Unless it be a virtue to possess,
Of "general cussedness," a trifle less

XVI.

Than some one else can boast of. "You stay here,
  And hold the team," he said, and through the door,
Regardless of the chilly atmosphere
  The horse and Will were in, he quickly bore
His heavy sack of corn, and laid it near
  The place for grinding it, upon the floor;
And by the fire he took a vacant seat,
And on the genial stove hearth warmed his feet.

XVII.

But Will was sitting where the wind swept past,
  In frigid waves, across the open space
Before the door, to which he often cast
  His eyes, while covering his ears and face:

The white horse shivered in the northern blast,
    And fain would have resumed the rapid pace,
Which brought her from the farm: and thus they stood,
Resisting for a while, as best they could,

XVIII.

The piercing wind and cold; but then it chanced
    Lorenzo Webb came also to the mill,
And on the platform threw his grist, and glanced
    His eyes around, and recognizing Will,
Who lived in his own neighborhood, advanced
    And said, in tones of kindness such as thrill
The heart, "My boy, what keeps you sitting there?"
"Fon left me," he replied, "to hold the mare."

XIX.

The oath Ren used I must forbear to print,
    Because of its apparent roughness, though
I hold there was a native virtue in't
    I should commemorate; at least I trow
The feeling prompting it, in virtue's mint,
    Had honestly been coined; and this I know,
That it was vigorous, if not refined;
And that to Will, his acts were very kind.

XX.

He took the horse, when he had tied his own,
    And, gently patting her upon the head —
An act of kindness she had seldom known —
    He led her to the almost empty shed,
Which fronted to the south, and having thrown
    A blanket over her, he turned and said,
"Now you get out, my lad," addressing Will,
"I think we'll find it warmer in the mill."

XXI.

He took Will's hand and led him to the door,
  And entered quietly and looked around,
And saw Alfonso sitting there before
  The fire, and seeming not to catch the sound
Of their approach; but slowly humming o'er,
  In sweet content and happiness profound,
Some plaintive snatches of an old love strain,
He watched the hopper jolting out the grain.

XXII.

Ren's eyes flashed fire at such a sight as this,
  While Will stood shivering in his kind embrace;
His teeth were set, he was about to hiss
  His righteous wrath into the miscreant's face;
But fearing he should thereby nearly miss
  The opportunity, by God's good grace
Presented — as he thought he could discern —
His course assumed a more heroic turn.

XXIII.

There lay upon the floor near where they stood,
  A pile of empty bags, from which he took
As many as conveniently he could,
  And wield them handily, and with a look
Of strong determination such as would
  No fear or hesitation ever brook,
He glided swiftly up behind the chair,
Where Fon was singing his pathetic air.

XXIV.

And swinging them aloft, above his head,
  With strength of muscle and of rage combined,
His clumsy weapon through its circle sped,
  And swift descended, as he had designed,

Upon his victim. There was nothing said,
  Before the blow, and naught, as I can find,
Was sung thereafter of his old love ditty,
  The loss of which I deem the greatest pity.

XXV.

Fon had received a pretty solid blow,
  As in his wrath, Lorenzo had intended ;
The weapon used, though awkward, wielded so,
  Had through the air quite rapidly descended ;
The straw hat which he wore was driven low
  Upon his face, till both must needs be mended —
At least the hat was torn, the forehead scratched,
The nose was bleeding and the skin detached.

XXVI.

"There," muttered Ren, "take that, you ugly cuss"—
  And was preparing quickly to repeat
The blow ; but here the miller, seeing the fuss,
  Ran towards the scene, and Fon sprang to his feet,
And stood a moment, then all tremulous,
  Sank down again in seemingly complete
Exhaustion ; so he deemed that he had done
Enough already ; and the battle won.

XXVII.

But Fon recovered quickly from the shock,
  And in a trice was on his feet again,
And — this time standing firmly as a rock —
  In anger and surprise said, "That you, Ren?"
As Cæsar did to Brutus, come to mock
  His former loyalty and friendship ; then,
Preparing to adopt a more aggressive
Defence, as 'twere, used language more expressive

XXVIII.

Than complimentary; but here anon,
  The miller interfered to keep the peace,
And learning of the facts, remarked to Fon
  'Twas lucky if he got so cheap release,
As now to call it even; whereupon
  Contention came to gradually cease,
Except the war of words ('twas not logomachy),
As venomous and bitter as *nux vomica*.

XXIX.

For Ren upbraided him in bitter terms,
  For his neglect and utter heartlessness —
Which oftener than else, perhaps, confirms
  The selfish passions, though to make them less,
Was his endeavor; to excite the germs
  Of love and kindness; and with such success,
On this occasion, that he offered Will
A dime, while going home, to keep it still.

XXX.

George Hayden worked with Fon one summer when
  About fifteen, but he had great capacity
For fighting; and his rights, 'gainst boys and men,
  He could defend with vigor and sagacity;
And if oppressed too sorely by him, then
  He would report him; and for strict veracity,
He had a reputation such as would
Establish what he said, for ill or good.

XXXI.

Fon thought one autumn day when he had dined,
  A short post-prandial nap would do him good;
At least he felt so sleepily inclined
  To take one, he determined that he would;

And so, to thoroughly relieve his mind
  Of all its worldly cares, and lest he should
Remain too long within the dream-god's bower,
He ordered George to wake him in an hour.

XXXII.

George knew that he'd been out the night before,
  And he had asked permission to go too,
Which Fon refused, and vehemently swore
  If he attempted it he'd " put him through "—
And now, to pay for this, or some old score,
  He thought 'twould be a cunning thing to do,
To overdo his part, and waken him
A little sooner; and, to serve his whim,

XXXIII.

He went and shook him, as he called out, " Fon ! "
  Which had but slight effect. He seemed to snore
Less loudly for an instant, then went on,
  About the same as he had done before.
" Fon ! Fon ! " he cried, " the time is almost gone,
  For you have now but fifteen minutes more ; "
Which seemed to rouse him from his sleep, and what
He said and did, I know, although 'tis not,

XXXIV.

Perhaps, worth while to fully specify,
  Except to say that he was pretty mad,
And went for George, demanding fiercely why
  The —— naming one whose fame is rather bad —
He didn't keep away and let him lie
  Until the time was up, and he had had
His full hour's sleep. He gave the order then,
" Hitch up the team ; " and went to sleep again.

XXXV.

George went and hitched the horses to the plow,
  Which Fon had held, and to redeem his joke,
He held himself, the best that he knew how,
  And drove the team — as gentle as a yoke
Of oxen, treated well, as they were now —
  For near another hour, when Fon awoke,
And came into the field; and when he saw
What George had done, he simply said, "*March donc!*"

XXXVI.

As Frenchmen do, and seized the plow again,
  And ordered George to "put 'em to their paces,"
And "put 'em through," — in seeming anger then,
  Without much cause, as frequently the case is —
And, oft with phrases ending in m-n
  (He didn't cultivate the Christian graces
To any great extent), he tore around,
Till nearly night, then, rusting in the ground,

XXXVII.

He left the plowshare, and unhitched the team,
  And took away from George the reins and whip,
And swung the latter in the sunset gleam,
  The former o'er his neck for surer grip; —
The nettled steeds, enveloped in the steam
  Of sweat and foam, again were made to sip
The cup of needless suffering and woe,
Which brutal men so oft on them bestow.

XXXVIII.

O foul brutality! thou art the worst
  Of all the varied forms of passion's mystery;
Thy cruel practices have ever cursed
  The world since first it had a written history:

And doubtless long before, when man was first
    Adjudged in righteousness by heaven's consistory,
Thy savage deeds were duly noted down,
And thou condemned by God's eternal frown.

XXXIX.

Thou art almost a universal crime;
" Man's inhumanity to man " alone,
" Makes countless thousands mourn " in every clime,
    And all the wide world o'er the poor brutes moan,
In needless wretchedness. A pantomime
    Of deeds for which the world cannot atone,
Has been enacted through the weary years,
And marked by brutish blood and human tears.

XL.

I knew a man whose lands were rich and wide,
    And in a cold northwestern climate lay,
Whose many cattle used to breast the tide
    Of dreadful winter by his stacks of hay,
Unsheltered from the wind, which pierced the hide,
    And flesh, and bone, and marrow, day by day,
Whose piteous lowing and whose plaintive cry,
Were almost constant as I passed them by.

XLI.

The brutes at length succumbed to nature's law,
    Their owner, long since dead, received his meed,
For want came first, to ravenously gnaw
    His shrivelled flesh; his substance gone to feed
A wealthy usurer's capacious maw,
    A modern Shylock's most insatiate greed —
More cruel than the winds and bitter cold —
Which vainly seeks to quench the thirst for gold.

XLII.

I've seen a Christian kneel and heard him say,
  "O Lord, we thank thee for our daily bread;"
While in his stable, thirty yards away,
  There stood a horse that just as plainly said,
"O pious master, give to me I pray,
  Some hay and oats;" but he received instead,
The galling collar and the cruel goad,
Until he fell exhausted at his load.

XLIII.

I heard a woman say — a preacher's wife —
  That where she came from they had "lots of fun,"
By getting up a "very unique" strife —
  By putting "scarecrow horses" on a run,
At county fairs — they having "scarcely life
  Enough to get there" — when the setting sun
Looked on a scene of great barbarity,
Which people loved apparently to see.

XLIV.

Well, "there must be an end to all careers,"
  Especially to those which sadly lack
Intelligence and virtue; as appears
  From what occurred when "the old man" got back,
As this Alphonso called in early years,
  His honored sire. He seemed to have the knack
Of being disrespectful to superiors,
Besides his great oppression of inferiors.

XLV.

While thus he drove the horses to the barn,
  George following behind and looking on,
Half angry with himself, and saying, "Darn
  A fellow that will be as mean as Fon" —

Without a premonition sent to warn
   Of danger from his father, who'd been gone,
That personage appeared upon the scene,
In time to see what Fon designed to screen

XLVI.

From observation of the parent's eye —
   For he supposed that he was still away —
By telling George to rub the horses dry,
   And put them in their stalls, and give them hay.
The father was expected late, and why
   He'd come so soon, Alphonso couldn't say,
But when he saw him, did the best he might,
To get into the stable, out of sight.

XLVII.

He knew from his experience before,
   The many faults a parent's love condones,
But now his father, rushing to the door,
   Exclaimed, " What means all this?" in thunder tones;
Which startled and surprised him vastly more
   Than thunder would. He shivered in his bones;
For well he knew there was sufficient cause
For great displeasure, if there ever was.

XLVIII.

He hesitated, stammered, tried to calm
   The horses down by gently saying whoa,
And wiped the foam from off them with the palm
   Of either hand, endeavoring to show
A seeming kindness, which should be a balm
   For righteous anger, though he didn't know
Exactly what to do or what to say ;
But said the horses " tried to run away."

XLIX.

The father called to George, who stood just through
 The door between the stable and the shed,
"Have you been driving in the same way too,
 And did the horses try to run?" he said.
"Yes," answered George, "they tried to run, 'tis true,
 But they were only jumpin' round, instead;
They would have run, for when he licked 'em so,
 They couldn't help it if he'd let 'em go."

L.

The father questioned further in the case,
 And listened patiently to such replies
As either made, whereon to fairly base
 A judgment that should be both just and wise;
Then looked Alphonso sternly in the face,
 And said, with husky voice and moistened eyes,
While Fon looked silently upon the floor,
"You needn't drive my horses any more.

LI.

"'Twill be six months before you're one-and-twenty,
 And even then you needn't go away,
But of your services I've had a plenty;
 Your time is yours, and you can go or stay."
He said it firmly, quite as if he meant he
 Should understand 'twas not mere children's play,
Then said to George, "You help me and we'll try
 If we can get these horses clean and dry."

LII.

O tyranny of kings! the earth has groaned
 Beneath thy sway for many thousand years;
And every nation which thy power has owned,
 Has paid the forfeit with a nation's tears;

Until advancing freedom has dethroned
  The sceptred tyrant, sounding in his ears,
The knell of power — the doom to which he must
  At length succumb — which Heaven pronounces just.

LIII.

And thou, the tyranny of human vice!
  More terrible than that which priest or king
Has ever exercised. Thou dost entice
  Thy subjects by false promises, to bring
Allegiance to thy crown. The fearful price
  Which they must pay therefor, includes the sting
Of wounded conscience, and the breaking down
Of manhood, and the loss of fair renown.

LIV.

Alphonso went away, the truth to tell,
  And went from bad to worse; and by degrees
His vices grew until he helped to swell
  The list of drunkards and of debauchees;
Though what, in later years, his life befell,
  I cannot say, his habits being these,
But look for reformation, near or far,
By nature's methods, whatsoe'er they are,

WILLOUGHBY'S WISDOM.

CANTO THIRD.

I.

About this time, as weather prophets say,
   I mean the ones who make the almanacs,
Or prophesy therein, in such a way
   As (though their augury all knowledge lacks)
To render difficult the proof that they,
   In their pretensions, are the merest quacks —
"Look out for storms about this time," the phrase
Strung up and down the margin thirty days.

II.

About this time, that is to say, about
   The time Alphonso came to his majority,
By somewhat prematurely wiping out
   The few remaining months of a minority
Wherein much virtue had been put to rout —
   About this time, or claiming slight priority,
George Hayden, fond of such amusements then,
Had found a place to play old sledge again.

III.

There lived in their immediate neighborhood,
   A married couple of young people who
Were fond of games; and who, whene'er they could,
   Invited others in that liked them too:

And George and Will, who partly understood
    The game they played the most, were often, through
Politeness or convenience, asked to come,
And take a hand, and thus were playing some.

IV.

I say young people, they were thirty, more
    Or less, their manners being rather free
And easy. Though respectable, they wore
    Their moral garments with some slight degree
Of comfort in the fit. He sometimes swore,
    In mild and moderate phrase, and even she,
Though kind and neighborly, was less refined
Than we would like to see all humankind.

V.

But Mrs. Smith — I like the name of Smith;
    Some people like a thing because it's odd;
And some have even worshipped but a myth,
    By some queer name, believing it a god.
Smith isn't odd, but rather claims its kith
    And kin 'mong all mankind; and gives its nod
Of recognition, at the least among
All nations of the English-speaking tongue.

VI.

This Mrs. Smith, whose father now was old,
    Had made a home for him, and he was there.
His wife had gone to where the streets are gold,
    And where celestial music fills the air.
And he could not approve of such a bold
    And reckless innovation, in the glare
Of gospel light, which he interpreted,
All mirthful pleasures strictly to forbid.

VII.

And Uncle Joe, as people called him then,
  Though deaf, decrepit and enfeebled so
He didn't mingle with his fellow men,
  As he had done in days of long ago,
Now grasped his cane and took his feet again,
  And walked abroad, to let a neighbor know
That his two boys had thus incurred the blame
Of playing there at this pernicious game.

VIII.

And Mr. Hayden, ere he went away,
  Politely thanked him for the information;
As, having children, we would do if they
  Were getting into mischief, or flirtation
With some forbidden sin, whose subtle sway
  Of evil threatened them with ruination;
But I should fear from Mr. Smith's profanity,
Much more than from the pleasure or the "vanity"

IX.

Of playing seven-up; and from the lack
  Of culture and refinement on the part
Of Mrs. Smith — whose manners seemed to smack
  Of native rudeness rather than the art
Of true politeness — more than from a pack
  Of cards; though she, I think, was good at heart,
But not well qualified to teach a boy,
By all the means which culture might employ.

X.

The next day after Uncle Joe had been
  To visit Mr. Hayden with design
Of telling him the news, as Will came in
  From playing ball — which stood in moral line —

He found his mother ready to begin
    A lecture, which he couldn't well decline
To listen to, without a violation
Of what he deemed was filial obligation.

XI.

She said she'd heard some news about him which
    Was very bad, provided it were true;
And in the story there was scarce a niche,
    Wherein to place a doubt. "I hear that you
And George," she said — and here she dropped a stitch,
    As she was taking hastily a few,
To where the knitting also might be dropped,
The " middle of the needle," where she stopped.

XII.

"I hear that you and George," continued she,
" While up at Mr. Smith's the other night,
Were playing cards; which quite surprises me,
    As you've been taught that playing isn't right,
Although 'tis true that they might not agree
    With us and with our teaching, which is quite
As worthy though, of your consideration,
As that of people who have no relation

XIII.

" With church or Sunday school, and who are not
    Converted to the righteous law of God;
And never had experience in what
    The Christian knows so well, who long has trod
The 'narrow way' which every person ought
    To walk in, rather than the one so broad,
And crowded with the many who, therein,
Are boon companions in the ways of sin."

XIV.

Will now was twelve, or "going on thirteen,"
  And though he had no strictly moral ground,
Whereon to make defence against the keen
  Assaults of wisdom, more or less profound,
He'd come to entertain, from what he'd seen,
  Of human nature and of "things around,"
A feeling that his mother was in error,
In vesting simple games with such a terror.

XV.

He made no very subtle argument,
  Nor any effort to conceal the fact:
He simply said he had no wrong intent,
  In doing what appeared a harmless act,
That when he went to Mr. Smith's, he went
  Because George did; and played because they lacked,
By one, the number it required to play;
And when the game was ended, came away.

XVI.

"But this," observed his mother, "isn't all,
  For Uncle Joe went on to say that when
The Smiths received from you and George, a call,
  George took the cards from his own pocket; then,
As unconcerned as you'd bring in your ball,
  When you were through, he put them in again,
As being his. Now is it true that he
Would buy such things, all unbeknown to me?"

XVII.

Will hesitated slightly, then replied,
  "He'd have to buy 'em when you didn't know
About it if he bought 'em, and to hide
  'Em somewhere when he didn't want 'em, so

You wouldn't make a fuss; and so he tried
  To keep it still; and would if Uncle Joe
Had staid at home and 'tended to his own
Affairs, and let the rest of us alone."

XVIII.

The anxious mother queried further still,
  As some particulars were yet in doubt;
Asked how they learned the game, and played it till
  It had so unexpectedly leaked out;
And said, continuing, " Now tell me, Will,
  How such a thing should ever come about,
That George should own the cards. Where did he buy
Them, where thus keep them hid away so sly?"

XIX.

"I s'pose," said Will, " he kept 'em in his chest,
  Or somewhere round up stairs, where he could find
'Em any time" — not deeming it were best
  To be explicit, but to rather blind
His mother's eyes, lest she should be in quest
  Of them as contraband, and be inclined
To burn them up, or put them where they might
Be difficult to find another night.

XX.

And also with the hope to thus evade
  The other question she had asked him, who
George had them of; which doubtless would have made
  The greatest difficulty of the two,
If it were answered fairly; so he paid
  But little heed to that, except to do
His utmost to prevent its further mention,
By otherwise diverting her attention.

XXI.

And he in this, succeeded very well ;
  The question wasn't then repeated ; so
He didn't have to answer it, or tell
  Of whom were bought the ugly chattels, though
He knew just where the whole transaction fell,
  But much preferred his mother shouldn't know ;
And so he went, with filial love sincere,
And kissed her cheek, whereon remained a tear.

XXII.

George then was serving out — no, that would be
  A violation of the etiquette,
Which treated all as seeming equals; he
  Was working out, as is the wording yet,
In this old commonwealth, where all are free,
  In fact, " where freedom's star has never set,"
It being after young Alphonso left,
Of his good name and legacy bereft.

XXIII.

And George was there, some eighty rods away,
  And coming home that night, was notified
That some important accusations lay
  Against him; and the case would then be tried.
Of course they'd ask him what he had to say,
  And if he pleaded guilty, woe betide,
If not, sufficient proof was, pro and con,
Already taken to convict him on.

XXIV.

The father was the formidable judge,
  And jury, witness and attorney ; and
With moral stamina that wouldn't budge
  An inch from justice, took the case in hand.

He showed no anger, prejudice or grudge,
　　And yet the " criminal " could understand
That 'twas in sober earnest, though for what
He'd been indicted, he as yet could not.

XXV.

Said Mr. Hayden, " Sir, I hear that you
　　Are owner of a pack of cards. If so,
Go bring them here, that we may have a view
　　Of Satan's pictured implements, and know
Just what we have to fight against." George drew
　　The cards from out his pocket ; which, although
He had demanded them, with some surprise,
　　The father saw produced before his eyes.

XXVI.

" Where did you get them ? " next demanded he,
　　" And when," he also asked, " did you begin
To play with them, without consulting me ;
　　Without your mother's knowing what was in
Your head or in your pocket ? Haven't we
　　Advised you constantly against the sin
Of playing wicked games, the danger too,
Of being ruined by them ere you're through ? "

XXVII.

" I haven't played but little," George replied,
　　" I bought the cards in trading with a boy,
In swapping knives and two three things beside,
　　He threw them in, because they might annoy " —
" Who was the boy ? " the father fiercely cried,
　　" Who was it thus all virtue would destroy ? "
" They might annoy his " — " Who ? " he thundered still,
　　" Who was the boy you traded with ? "—" ' *Twas Will.*"

XXVIII.

O sinful pleasure! thou hast held thy sway,
 O'er human hearts, and often hast laid waste
The fairest temples ever made of clay,
 Since Eve and Adam, upright, pure and chaste,
First welcomed thee. Let's see, what did they say?
 'Twas " good for food," and pleasant to the taste —
Or rather it was " pleasant to the eyes,"
And was " to be desired to make them wise."

XXIX.

It has been said thy votaries are fools;
 That " he that loveth pleasure shall be poor; "
And here are two lads trading in the tools
 Of pleasure's workshop; but the next detour
May see them sit in sorrow on the stools
 Of penance; whereon every great wrong doer
Must sooner sit or later, ere his sin
Be blotted out and happiness begin.

XXX.

Now here was what might well be deemed a fix,
 Especially for Will, whom George had tried,
By silence and evasion, not to mix
 With his shortcomings when he had replied,
Until his father had so trumped his tricks,
 That he, unless he positively lied,
At length had been compelled to own that they
Had trafficked some in that forbidden way.

XXXI.

The case was tried, the verdict duly rendered,
 By full confessions made by the accused;
Some little bitterness had been engendered,
 By ugly facts and by the methods used

To find them. George was generously tendered
   His choice — whereat he felt somewhat confused —
Between " a whipping " and the confiscation
Of all the cards, with promised reformation.

XXXII.

He would quite willingly have sacrificed
   The pack of cards, an old pack any way,
But such a promise as he was advised
   To make, and pledge himself he wouldn't play,
Was one which, as he reasoned, compromised
   Too much of freedom at a future day; —
And being whipped, as cannot be denied,
If not unjust, would be undignified.

XXXIII.

"Well, there's the cards," he said, "and you can do
   Just what you like with them, and " — here was heard
A loud rap on the door; and guessing who
   'Twas given by, wherein he hadn't erred —
Although he didn't guess the business too,
   Whereon he came — the father gave the word,
"Come in," and Deacon Alden swung the door,
And was surprised at what he stood before.

XXXIV.

For Mr. Hayden still was sitting by
   The table which the cards were lying on,
And George was sitting opposite; his eye,
   The deacon thought, with seeming gladness shone;
While Mrs. H. and Will, a little shy,
   (It might be so) had just got up and gone;
As if they'd recently been playing there,
A sort of private, family affair.

XXXV.

The deacon, when he entered, also had,
  Along with him, two other persons who,
Or one of whom, was feeling rather bad,
  About some late mishap. The other too,
Though less unfortunate, was looking sad,
  And wondering what the deacon meant to do:
The one was Nathan and the other Tim —
Tim Turner — and the others met with him,

XXXVI.

But just outside the door; for he had come,
  As by his mother's leave, to stay with Will,
That night, he being Will's familiar chum,
  A place he seemed well qualified to fill,
Their friendship being constant, saving some
  Slight disagreements, such as children still —
Some older people too, I grieve to say —
Are troubled with, in that same childish way.

XXXVII.

And meeting Nathan as they neared the house,
  Nate told him in a whisper by the door,
His father had come up, "as still's a mouse,"
  And caught them "playin' jacks" the night before.
He grabbed the cards and said he'd bet a grouse
  They wouldn't play with that pack any more,
And when he told him George and Will played too,
He said, "We'll see to-morrow if they do."

XXXVIII.

And there they were; and when the deacon saw
  The cards upon the table lying there,
It so surprised him he could scarcely draw
  His breath for half a minute. "I declare!"

Said he, "Have you amended Heaven's law,
 Or have you broken it; or do things wear
A false appearance? Tell me which or what;
Have you been playing cards, or have you not?"

XXXIX.

"No, Deacon," Mr. Hayden answered, "no,
 We've not been playing, I at least have not,
Nor have I ever taught my children so,
 But George and Will have somehow, lately, got
Bewitched with them, and have been led to go
 Where people play; and they've played too, and what
Were right and best, in such a case, to do,
I was debating; but was nearly through,

XL.

"When you came in. Now what if your boy here,
 Not quite as old as George, had done the same,
And if, on questioning, it should appear
 The cards were his, and"—"That's just what I came
For," here broke in the deacon, "and I fear
 My boy than yours is not much less to blame—
To ask of you the question you ask me;
And tell you what I found last evening; see!"

XLI.

And thereupon, with looks a little sad,
 He drew another pack from out his pocket,
And laid it down. Tim whispered, "That's too bad."
 And Mr. Hayden's face expressed the shock it
Produced upon him when he saw they had
 Another case for trial on the docket;
With the respondent waiting at the bar
Of justice, as all human beings are.

XLII.

Not many questions did they ask of Nate,
  The deacon told the story, how he found
Him in his room up stairs, a little late,
  The night before, attracted by the sound
Of undertones, which showed he had a mate,
  And as he knew another boy was round,
A little earlier, but thought he'd gone,
He went to his apartment, whereupon,

XLIII.

He found them both. The other boy and he,
  Were busy playing there at high-low-jack;
A sorry sight it grieved his heart to see,
  To discontinue which, he seized the pack;
And now had come to see what course should be
  Pursued concerning those who seemed to lack
Appreciation of the teaching they
Had been accustomed to from day to day.

XLIV.

As all the facts had now been laid before
  Them, it remained to say what should be done;
And Mr. Hayden, much in earnest, wore
  A solemn look, as when he had begun;
But by and by there suddenly came o'er
  The deacon's face a somewhat different one;
A sort of twinkle of the eye, in fact,
As if he had a thought the other lacked.

XLV.

"I'll tell you, neighbor," he remarked, "what we
  May safely do with these two packs of cards;
Let's play a game, two handed, you and me,
  Or play four-handed, you and I be 'pards,'

'Gainst George and Nathan. Will and Tim can be
    A sort of umpires, referees, or guards,
To see fair play; and when the game is done,
All say that this shall be the final one.

XLVI.

"Come," he continued, with a sturdy grace,
    Removing from the table to the fire,
And sitting down, "come, here's a handy place,
    Where none need take the trouble to inquire
Who played the highest card, as even the ace
    Will save no trick, but find its funeral pyre,
Here on the hearth; and Heaven grant that we,
No fiercer flames than these, may ever see."

XLVII.

'Twill be remembered George was broken in
    Upon in his reply concerning whether
He would consent to sacrifice the sin
    Of playing with them, and the cards together,
Or take the consequences he had been
    So threatened with, from stick or strap of leather;
And thinking he'd accept the first condition,
His father yielded to the proposition

XLVIII.

The deacon made; and sitting down by him,
    And taking both the packs, began to shuffle;
For he regarded it a harmless whim,
    And in his temper there was scarce a ruffle:
They all maintained their gravity but Tim,
    And he was civil, but he had to muffle
A tendency to laughter all the while,
Expressing only an incipient smile.

XLIX.

George said he guessed he wouldn't take a part
   In that game if he couldn't play again;
Not being well acquainted with the art,
   He'd let the "final game" be played by men;
Whereby he artfully designed to start
   A false impression, to the end that when
The cards were gone, his father wouldn't press
A more decisive answer, no or yes.

L.

Well, Mr. Hayden shuffled, as I said,
   And dealt the cards by handing over some
To his companion, when the deacon led,
   By taking 'twixt his fingers and his thumb,
A queen of hearts, which to the flames so red,
   He then consigned, and for all time to come;
As from the fervent heat and ruddy flame,
Its former self no power could reclaim.

LI.

"Depart ye cursed," Mr. Hayden cried —
   As on the deacon's card, or after it,
He threw another to the burning tide —
   "To everlasting fire" — in language fit
For such occasion — "and therein abide,
   Where you no further evil may commit."
And thus their game they reverently played,
Though even they grew jovial as they made

LII.

Some farther progress. All are apt to, who
   Indulge in games, the cares of life to bury,
In brief forgetfulness, when they are through —
   It is their province thus to make us merry;

And why about it make so much ado?
   'Tis better far than drinking hock and sherry —
And 'tis a world we must be jolly in,
   At times, though full of sorrow and of sin.

LIII.

I say this as a truth, and in defence
   Of Mr. Hayden and the deacon. They,
However, played but once, and in a sense
   Somewhat Pickwickian, to throw away
Some cards which had offended them; and hence
   Might not be reckoned players; but I say
That if they touched a sad or humorous strain,
They only hoped a righteous end to gain.

LIV.

"Remember, Deacon, that I've played the ace."
   Said Mr. Hayden, "which you know is high — "
"And will be higher soon, for I can trace
   It in the smoke ascending to the sky,"
The deacon answered, "but you know the race,
   Or who has won it fairly, by and by,
Must be determined by the count; and then
If you should have the ace or deuce, or ten

LV.

To count for game, we'll reckon in a lump,
   What each one is, by what he has to show;
And if you've nothing then, you're up a stump,
   And cannot claim the jack or high or low; — "
"It's your play, Deacon, follow suit or trump,"
   Broke in the other, and they seemed to know
Some little of the nomenclature, which
Surprised the boys, each sitting in his niche,

LVI.

And watching closely as the game went on,
　　Until they stood, or claimed to stand, "two and;"
But by and by the deacon's cards were gone,
　　While Mr. Hayden still had some in hand,
From which at once the other would have "drawn,"
　　Until the players should again command
An equal number, as was sometimes done,
Although the rule was not a legal one.

LVII.

But Tim remembered what the deacon said,
　　When he devised the present clever way,
By which the boys to virtue should be led,
　　That he and Will should see they had fair play;
So looking up and stretching up his head,
　　He raised a point of rule as follows: "Say,
You can't do that way, as I understand,
You've made a misdeal. You must pack the hand."

LVIII.

The deacon smiled, although he felt inclined,
　　Against his umpire's ruling to protest;
And so he drew, as he at first designed,
　　A card or two, but Tim had had his jest,
As well as they; and that they didn't mind,
　　But couldn't "pack the hand," so played the rest,
And Mr Hayden said, "We're two and two,
I think, and guess for us one hand will do."

IX.

The deacon took from out his wallet then,
　　Some silver coins, and said, "I'll tell you what:
If you, my lads, will now behave like men,
　　And promise me that henceforth you will not

Possess a card, or play with them again,
    I'll give you what they cost when they were bought,"
Selecting what he judged — two ninepences —
Would pay George for his pack, and Nate for his.

LX.

Poor Nathan felt constrained to answer yes,
    And took the cash his father would bestow;
But I have known a yes which promised less
    Of good achievement than an honest no;
As did the man who would his sons impress,
    To labor in his vineyard once. "I go,"
Said one — but didn't — when the two were bid,
The other said he wouldn't go, but did.

LXI.

George said, "I thank you, but will not accept
    The money for them, as the cards were old —
Old when I got them, for they had been kept
    Among the boys, and had been bought and sold,
Good many times;" wherein he overstepped
    The truth but slightly if at all, but told
It pretty nearly as it was, as Will
Had got them where they had been used until

LXII.

The older boys thought they would hardly do
    For them to deal and shuffle any more,
And so when, recently, one of them who
    Had owned them, got some new ones at the store,
And as he didn't need or care for two,
    Will bought them for a trifle, just before
They went at first to Mr. Smith's and played,
And then to George he sold them in a trade.

LXIII.

The deacon chatted for a little while —
   Perhaps for thirty minutes, more or less —
Of heaven's mercy and of Satan's guile,
   But said no more to George to further press
The subject of the promise. With a smile,
   He rose to go, and George remarked, "I guess
I'll go with them;" and bidden not, to stay,
By father or by mother, went away.

LXIV.

Then Will was questioned as to how he came
   To own the cards, and when he told them how,
'Twas not so damaging to his good fame,
   As they had thought, or feared at least, just now;
And yet they held that he was much to blame,
   For having them at all; and asked a vow
Of reformation, which he partly gave,
But managed so to word it as to save

LXV.

His conscience, should he chance to play again,
   Or own another pack some future day;
Although he saw no likelihood just then,
   Of doing either, as the fates said nay;
But he and George would sometime both be men,
   And then, he thought, could have it their own way;
Although of what he thought he nothing said,
And he and Tim then went up stairs to bed.

LXVI.

And so the matter dropped, and George and Will
   Abstained from playing cards the winter through;
And Nathan's money he had kept until
   The spring returned, and till his father, who

Had often asked him if he had it still,
  Had somehow seemingly forgotten to
Repeat the question; taking it for granted
  That now the cards were thoroughly supplanted.

LXVII.

But in the spring a peddler came along,
  And overtaking Nate upon the way,
He asked the boy to ride; nor deemed it wrong,
  To ask him further if he didn't play
At games of cards. "I'll sell you for a song,"
  He patronizingly went on to say,
"This nice new set for playing high-low-jack;"
As, saying which, he handed him the pack.

LXVIII.

The cards were new, but rather thin and light,
  A fact which Nate, however, didn't see.
He was debating whether now he might
  Become their owner, if they could agree
Upon the price. He knew it wasn't quite
  The proper thing to do, nor would it be
A safe procedure, under circumstances
So full of danger, thus to take the chances

LXIX.

Of being known to have the cards again,
  Or short in his accounts. His "cash in hand"
Would not hold out if he invested then
  To the amount the other would demand,
And yet like other boys, and many men,
  In such positions, he could not withstand
The sore temptation, and he asked the price,
Unmindful of his father's sage advice.

LXX.

O broken promise! if thou hadst been kept,
    In every case wherein thou hast been broken,
How much less frequently had maiden wept,
    Or parent mourned; for thou hast been the token
Of every vice, while every virtue slept,
    Although thy words had been sincerely spoken;
Or more or less so at the least, as when
Nate promised he would not play cards again.

LXXI.

O breach of trust! how oft hast thou betrayed
    The misplaced confidence of guileless men,
Who have their treasures indiscreetly laid
    In places whence they've not returned again.
Some well-known spendthrift often has been made
    A corporation treasurer, and then,
When he some cunning method has devised,
By which to swindle them, men seem surprised.

LXXII.

The peddler said, "I'm selling such as these,
    For twenty cents, but if you wish for one,
As you're a boy — I always like to please
    The little folks — and seeing we've begun
To make a trade, we'll change the fives to threes,
    And call it but a ninepence when we're done;
Or if you take two packs, we'll call them then
But twenty cents for two — each of them ten."

LXXIII.

They'd reached the place where George was living still —
    At Mr. Rollins', where he'd worked before —
And he'd been so promoted as to fill
    The place of foreman, held by Fon of yore,

Who now was roaming at his own sweet will,
    And didn't "plow and harrow any more,"
He said, but then he sowed "wild oats" instead,
And spent his money for what wasn't bread.

LXXIV.

And Nate proposed that he and George should buy
    The two, so they could have each of them one;
But George could see some weighty reasons why
    They shouldn't do it; and he meant to shun
The danger such a purchase would imply,
    Because he feared some mischief might be done,
If they should make a movement of the kind,
And so the proposition he declined.

LXXV.

And he reminded Nate that he had been
    Induced to promise that he wouldn't play,
And also that the cards were very thin,
    And "hardly worth a fo' pence any way;"
If he should buy them he'd get taken in —
    And find, perhaps, the dickens was to pay,
Before he knew it, as his father might
Get hold of them and him some other night.

LXXVI.

"Well, well, my lad," the peddler said to Nate,
    "Your purpose this young man shall not defeat;
For you shall have a pack at any rate,
    And have them for the same, which can't be beat
They're worth as much, I do not hesitate
    To say — this single pack, all clean and neat —
As I had asked you for the two, and yet
A dime makes you the owner of the set."

LXXVII.

" All right," said Nate, " I guess if you'll agree
  To never say a word, I'll take 'em whuther
George does or not." " You never fear for me,
  I'll keep as whist as a masonic brother,"
He said, and then the very coin which he
  Received as compensation for the other,
Nate handed him in payment for the pack,
Receiving for his change, two pennies back.

LXXVIII.

The peddler started off, and Nate said no,
  When asked if he'd get on the cart again,
He wasn't far from home, and wouldn't go
  The balance of the way, he guessed, just then,
He'd stay with George a little while, and so
  He held the plow for several furrows, when,
As George proposed to let the horses stand,
Nate asked him if he'd like to " try a hand."

LXXIX.

Said George, " You promised, if I recollect,
  You wouldn't buy or play ; but now I take it
That you've concluded 'twould be quite correct,
  No matter what your promise was, to break it."
" Who cares?" said Nate, "for how could he expect
  I'd keep the promise when I had to make it?"
And it must be conceded such a flaw
In the agreement might be held in law,

LXXX.

To be sufficient to obliterate
  The obligation. George could hardly say
But this new argument, thus raised by Nate,
  Had partially confirmed his right to play.

At any rate they didn't longer wait,
    For further questioning, but right away,
As if they were exempt from moral blame,
Sat on the plow beam and commenced a game.

LXXXI.

Meanwhile the peddler drove before the door,
    At Deacon Alden's, where he stopped to trade;
And wanting something she had not in store,
    The deacon's wife some little purchase made;
And he himself came in the house before
    'Twas done, at least before the bill was paid,
And handed out a dollar to the man,
Who drew from out his pocket, and began

LXXXII.

To count therefrom, a handful of small change;
    And looking on, the deacon chanced to see
A ninepence which he thought a little strange
    Of finding there, for he was sure that he
Remembered it; and wished he might arrange
    To get it; and it happened so to be,
That, making change, the trader gave him that,
Which holding fast and looking closely at,

LXXXIII.

He asked the peddler, "Can you tell me where
    You got this coin?" and then it flashed across
The other's mind. "Well, really, I declare,"
    He blandly said, "I'm no less at a loss
To know than you; in fact, I never care
    For that, I see if it is good, and toss
It in among the rest, then as before,
I go and see if I can get some more."

LXXXIV.

The deacon asked him further, if he'd seen,
  Within a mile or so of there, a lad ;
A stout built fellow of about fourteen :
  The peddler answered promptly that he had ;
"In fact," he said, "if there is naught between,
  I think I'll show him to you. Was he clad
In suit of kersey gray?" The deacon said
He was, and wore a cloth cap on his head.

LXXXV.

Then from a little peddler's trunk of tin,
  He drew a glass, of modest form and size —
Not such as men hold 'twix the nose and chin,
  An opera glass — and held it to his eyes ;
And looking south, he saw what would have been
  To Deacon Alden's sight, a sad surprise ;
For there they were, still sitting on the beam,
And playing high-low-jack to rest the team.

LXXXVI.

He looked some time, as if he hadn't found
  Just where they were, debating what to do ;
The deacon also sharply looked around,
  And with the naked eye could see them too ;
Could see at least, a black speck on the ground —
  Not what the peddler could when looking through
The glass — nor did the latter want he should,
And would prevent it somehow, if he could.

LXXXVII.

So he began to talk about the glass,
  Invented by Rinaldo, as he said,
Long years ago, through which to see, alas !
  What human eyes should have beheld with dread ;

What constituted then a numerous class
   Of cruel "sports," now fortunately dead;
Or mainly so at least, except in some
   More savage climes, where conscience still is dumb.

LXXXVIII.

"'Tis not so indispensable, 'tis true,
   As are the spectacles," continued he,
"Which people wear when old, or when, like you,
   Beginning to grow old, as all must be:
The Scripture says, 'The days of man are few — '"
   The deacon interrupted, "Let me see."
"Oh yes sir," said the other, "I will show
   You where they are, I think you'll see them, though

LXXXIX.

Some smoke has gathered in the atmosphere"
   (O would some friendly mantle always cloak us
Whene'er our sins are likely to appear,
   Or they be cancelled by some hocus-pocus);
"The glass, you'll see, will bring them pretty near — "
   But handing it, he turned it out of focus;
And in this unknown, unsuspected guise,
The deacon took, and raised it to his eyes.

XC.

He looked awhile, but didn't seem to find
   What he was looking for, and took it down.
"Perhaps 'tis true that I am getting blind,"
   He said, with half a smile and half a frown;
Then tried some views besides the one designed,
   And held it towards the mountain, bare and brown;
But all seen through it being misty, he,
Beginning to examine, said, "Let's see,

XCI.

Does this turn round, and out and in, or how?"—
  Invention of necessity is born—
And then he turned it once or twice, and now,
  On looking through, it seemed as clear as morn.
And he would soon have seen them on the plow,
  But there was heard the blowing of a horn;
Which brings good news alike to saint and sinner,
And this was blown for George to come to dinner.

XCII.

'Twas quite a little later than he thought,
  And so at once he sprang upon his feet;
For he had " rested " longer than he ought,
  And now must hurry round, and so complete
The present bout, returning to the spot
  Where he began each furrow to repeat—
And Nate picked up the cards and put them in
The pocket where his money should have been.

XCIII.

When Deacon Alden, sharply peering through
  The glass, discovered George and Nathan, they
Were up and doing what they had to do,
  Nate holding plow, endeavoring to lay
A handsome furrow; till it brought them to
  The corner, when their work, as well as play,
They there abandoned, and unhitched the plow,
And Nate walked homeward with a placid brow.

XCIV.

The deacon, turning to the peddler, said,
  " What did you sell the boy? this coin I gave
To him some months ago, when he'd been led
  Into an error which I sought to save

Him from, and teach him wisdom's ways instead."
The peddler, who was not an arrant knave,
But in expedients a little handy,
Said he had sold him nothing but some candy.

XCV.

And sure enough! when Nate came up the road,
He had a stick of candy in his hand
(That George had given him), which clearly showed
The peddler's yarn was not a rope of sand;
And yet the circumstances might forebode
Unfortunate *denouements*, which should strand
His barque of fiction on the rock of truth;
As oft has chanced to some ingenuous youth,

XCVI.

When things were not what they appeared to be;
But this was probable at any rate,
The facts and statement seeming to agree;—
"Hello, my lad," the peddler said to Nate,
"I've something here perhaps you'd like to see;"
And holding up the glass, went on to state
That that would bring far distant objects near;
Then placed it on his nose, while in his ear,

XCVII.

He whispered hastily, "You wait until
Your father goes away;" and asked him then,
Aloud, if he could see on yonder hill,
Some cattle, sheep or horses, dogs or men;
"Then take the glass," he said, "and hold it still,
And steady on your nose, and look again."
For Nate had answered there were none of these,
That all that he could see was stumps and trees.

XCVIII.

Nate took the glass, which had been held too high —
  His father stepped into the house a minute —
The peddler said, "You'll have to tell a lie
  About the cards, or else the deuce is in it;
In making change with him, it happened I
  A ninepence gave him, and as sure as sin it
Was yours; and so I said, to help you through,
You bought some candy. You can say so too."

XCVIX.

"Oh dear!" said Nate, "he knew how much I'd got,
  He'll know I wouldn't spend ten cents for that;
I wish you'd take 'em back, and give me what
  You can afford — what you can sell 'em at,
To any boy that plays, for like as not
  He'll want to see my money; then he'll bat
Me for it if it's gone, and I can't show
The candy either — and I can't you know."

C.

"All right," the peddler said, "I'll give you eight,
  And take them back, although you've played a game
Or two." "I'll do it; take 'em quick," said Nate,
  "'Fore he comes back;" and presently he came;
Though not till they'd had time to stipulate
  The terms of sale, and carry out the same,
And Nate had got his money in his pocket,
The secret locked so they could not unlock it.

CI.

The peddler gathered his commodities
  Into his cart, and slowly drove away:
And Nate was glad for what remained of his,
  Although at best he was compelled to say

That he was beaten — as he ever is
    Who plays unfairly in a moral play —
A play wherein poor Nate had lost a game,
But saved his reputation free from blame:

CII.

As many a worthy youth had done before —
    As many a man has done in later years;
As if he valued reputation more
    Than character, which afterwards appears;
And even through the masks the parties wore,
    In spite of all pretence, and all veneers —
Becomes as visible as sun or moon,
At noon of night or at the hour of noon.

WILLOUGHBY'S WISDOM.

CANTO FOURTH.

I.

Perhaps the reader may expect, ere long,
   Before the desultory tale advances
Much farther, that I'll weave into my song,
   Some record of the chances and mischances
Of youthful loves and lovers; such as throng
   The pages of old legends and romances:
But this is not designed to be a story,
Exclusively of love, or fame, or glory.

II.

And yet, if peradventure I should find
   My characters in love — or any one,
Or two or more of them — I shouldn't mind
   Recording all the facts, as I've begun
To write, and as I'm natively inclined
   To truth; so should it chance to sometimes run
In that direction, to a modest flame,
I shouldn't deem myself at all to blame.

III.

Will Hayden was enamored of his books,
   And also in a general way, of girls;
And there was one of whom he liked the looks,
   Much better than the rest; whose glossy curls

Afforded him some quite convenient nooks,
   Wherein to hide his fingers. As it whirls,
The wheel of fortune brings us all at times,
Within the spell of love's euphonious chimes.

IV.

And yet to Will his books were all in all,
   Or nearly so, for he was quite intent
On his emancipation from the thrall
   Of ignorance and error; and he meant,
At the academy, the coming fall,
   If so his father would give his consent,
To delve a little in the mysteries
Of education, which should thus be his.

V.

He now was working out upon a farm;
   Engaged for all the season, which would run
Some weeks beyond the date which held the charm
   Of being that when school should be begun:
But then he reckoned it would do no harm,
   If that could satisfactorily be done,
To shorten it by so much, as he could,
By teaching in the winter, make it good.

VI.

His age was then a little past eighteen;
   It so increases as the years extend.
We all grow old, as can be plainly seen;
   Our earthly pilgrimage will shortly end;
And we may look upon the silvery sheen,
   With which we gild, as lights and shadows blend,
The other shore; and fondly trust that 'tis
From intuition's truthful prophesies.

VII.

"That other shore, that mystic other shore!
  O who shall tell us of the great unknown?
Whose eye hath pierced its shadowy boundaries o'er,
  Whose feet have wandered in that fragrant zone?"*
'Tis true, alas! that those who've " gone before,"
  Have nearly all a solemn silence shown,
Although Judge Samuel appeared to Saul,
And truly prophesied his speedy fall.

VIII.

Will's father was an upright, honest man,
  But generosity had made him poor;
As he had signed some heavy notes, which ran
  To some old Shylock whom he would secure
Against the failure, by his brother Dan,
  To make the payment good; and to be sure,
Had all to pay; as I did when I went
To ride one day with dancing-master Brent.

IX.

A man of straw, as I have found, alas!
  Who dealt in patent rights; at least who bought
As many as he could of every class,
  But never sold them, though he always thought
Them all bonanzas, whence he should amass
  A fortune when his latest scheme was wrought
Completely out, as he should now begin it,
For he was sure that there were "millions in it."

X.

But Mr. Hayden lent a better name,
  For many times as much as I did mine,
The upshot of it being just the same,
  He had to pay to teach him not to sign;

---

* From " The Other Shore," by Laura Brigham Boyce.

And so from moderate independence, came
  Almost to penury, that foe malign!
Although his home had never been the haunt,
At any time, of grim and hungry want.

XI.

But he could not, perhaps, afford to pay
  Large sums for education — nor did he,
In fact, believe much in it any way,
  To any great extent, or high degree;
But always held, and often used to say,
  To "read and write and cipher," this should be
The aim of "common folks" in worldly lore,
Insisting that they needed nothing more.

XII.

And of his five now nearly grown up sons,
  No one had much rebelled against the rule,
Though one I think — one of the older ones —
  Had been a teacher in a district school,
Where little else, as education runs,
  Or did run then — unless 'twas playing "gool" —
Was ever taught to pupils but to pickle 'em
In Mr. Hayden's primitive curriculum.

XIII.

But Will did not believe in "common folks,"
  In such a sense that they should not aspire,
In spite of caste and her oppressive yokes,
  To something better and to something higher.
He deemed it quite legitimate to coax,
  From fickle fortune, all the heart's desire,
Or all at least, she could be made to give,
Of happiness and knowledge while we live.

XIV.

He furthermore believed that he could pay
   His bills, until he should be fairly learned,
If he could be allowed to have his way,
   And to appropriate what he had earned;
And also help to keep the wolf at bay,
   Beneath the parent roof; where he returned,
On many a sultry evening in July
And August, when the sun had left the sky,

XV.

To try to get his father to consent
   To let him go to school the coming fall,
But it was evident the father meant
   He shouldn't see a higher school at all,
Than that to which his elder brothers went,
   Commencing early, when almost too small
To go and come, thence up to one-and-twenty;
And this for learning he esteemed a plenty.

XVI.

Thus unsuccessful in his mission, Will
   Returned in sadness to the morrow's task;
And often on the way, when all was still,
   And earth was putting on her shadowy mask,
Sat on an old spruce log and wept, until
   He'd thought of some new form in which to ask
The same old question of his father, when
He should go home to plead his cause again.

XVII.

Nor was it ever many days before
   He reappeared, and standing at the bar
Of that paternal court to which, of yore,
   We all were held amenable, and are

Impressed with its solemnity as o'er
  The distant past, we see it from afar —
He advocated earnestly again,
  The rights of boys aspiring to be men.

XVIII.

And yet with him the court was always stern,
  And its decisions constantly adverse;
Until he came reluctantly to learn
  That they contained but little save the hearse
Of all his hopes and arguments, in turn,
  Which now began to rapidly disperse;
For he could see no way to re-begin
The suit there seemed so little chance to win.

XIX.

This was the second of the only two
  Great disappointments he had ever known;
The first occurring two years previous, through
  An unsuccessful effort of his own,
To go to dancing school, with others who,
  Of old Terpsichore's fine art, had grown
So fond; but he was destined then to be
Defeated by his father's stern decree.

XX.

And then he demonstrated his capacity
  To pay expenses, having wrought and schemed,
With all his energy, and some sagacity —
  Made extra efforts many times, which seemed
To promise well, and held with great tenacity,
  His small remunerations, till he deemed
He had a sum sufficient now to pay
His bills, which would be moderate any way.

XXI.

And when his scheme received its overthrow,
    A fate which somehow he did not expect,
He felt as if he couldn't have it so,
    And in it some injustice would detect:
He had his girl engaged, and he most go
    And tell her, and he feared it might reflect
Upon his constancy; but she, instead
Of so regarding it, most kindly said,

XXII.

" No matter Will, no matter, though 'tis true
    I feel the disappointment just the same,
Or none the less, I dare say, than do you,
    But then it can't be helped; you're not to blame.
Perhaps — " and here a longer breath she drew,
    But nothing further of the sentence came,
So what it would have been he had to guess—
A thought, perhaps, not prudent to express.

XXIII.

She had a brother two years older than
    Herself, she being just as old as Will;
And he one night, before the school began,
    As they were sitting by the window sill,
Said, I believe that I can lay a plan
    For Will to go, a while at least, until
He's learned some part of it, in spite of all
His Father's said and done. I'll go and call

XXIV.

Upon him soon, and say I'll come again,
    And he must come and visit you and me.
I'll tell him not to tell his father when
    The school is to begin, and, don't you see?

I'll have him come that very night, and then
    We'll hitch the old mare up, by hokey! he
And I, if we can make it work, and go;
    And soon we'll learn to shake the heel and toe."

XXV.

He did as he proposed, and early sought
    An interview with Will, and told him; though
The latter hesitated, as he ought,
    In view of such a firm paternal no,
As he'd received, and then besides, he thought
    'Twould be ungenerous in him to go,
And leave the girl behind, in such a way,
But she insisted that he shouldn't stay

XXVI.

On her account; that if he deemed it right,
    And would assume so much responsibility,
Or risk the chances that his father might
    Detect him in it, and his incivility,
Or disobedience, might then requite,
    By compromising his assumed gentility,
In such a way as should give cause to rue it,
Then she would do her best to help him through it.

XXVII.

So on the night in question, he and Frank —
    Her brother — started for the dancing hall,
And, having no experience, took their rank
    Among beginners, who were mostly small,
Which made them feel as if 'twere time they drank
    Of this peculiar pleasure, if at all —
And partly, to themselves, it justified
The very doubtful measure they had tried.

XXVIII.

They made good progress in the steps, however,
    And one or two could very fairly take,
Before the lesson closed; and they were clever
    In conversation, and they chanced to make
Some fond associations, which to sever,
    Caused "such emotions as the heart may break,"
If magnified sufficiently, although
It might require some thousand times or so.

XXIX.

Associations discontinued when
    The evening's lessons had been all gone through,
And practised once or twice apiece, for then,
    Like most of the aspiring youngsters who
Were there, the boys straightway returned again,
    And Will, as many boys are wont to do,
Endeavored to get in and not be heard —
To give no signal of what had occurred.

XXX.

What shadowy things seem real in a dream,
    In whose queer freaks we are but helpless toys:
A door, swung open in the night, will scream;
    To drive nails Sunday makes a dreadful noise.
At least such noises then much louder seem,
    To reverent men and late returning boys,
Who try into their rooms to softly creep,
And not disturb their mothers in their sleep.

XXXI.

And yet on this occasion Will succeeded
    In getting in unusually well;
He made no sound which he himself had heeded,
    So silently the door-latch rose and fell;

But some maternal hearts have nothing needed,
    At times, but presence, all doubts to expel;
As what his mother said might indicate,
"It seems to me you've staid out rather late."

XXXII.

She said no more, though he made no reply;
    She knew whom she addressed in tones so mild,
For while the father slept with heavy eye,
    The mother felt the presence of her child:
And yet she could not feel the untold lie,
    Or untold truth, by which she was beguiled —
Such are thy mysteries O nature! such,
O love! which tells so little and so much.

XXXIII.

Well, when the evening of the next week came,
    On which the dance was had, the two boys tried,
And tried successfully, to do the same
    That they had done before; and Will, to hide
His purposes, and shun apparent blame,
    Slipped out his Sunday clothes, securely tied
Into a bundle, while his "every day"
Ones he, to this same neighbor's wore away.

XXXIV.

The third week Mr. Hayden took a notion,
    However, Will should not go anywhere
That evening, raising thus a sad commotion,
    Within his breast, although 'twas not despair:
It simply acted as a cooling lotion,
    To spirits that were growing light as air,
In spite of disappointment, and in spite
Of even Fannie's staying every night,

XXXV.

At home, while helping him to get away —
  As was becoming in a neighbor's daughter,
To help a neighbor's son — and he, or they,
  To pay her for it, diligently taught her
What they had learned at night, the following day,
  And all the week; and Will I dare say thought her
As tractable a scholar as he could
Have had or wished; as any fellow would.

XXXVI.

That night, however, things were changed about:
  Will didn't come, although they knew not why;
And Frank proposed that she for once go out,
  And she was not unwilling to comply,
Although her mother did express some doubt
  If it were best, and yet she didn't try
To force compliance, and she went; and she
Taught Will that lesson, so he then had three.

XXXVII.

And when he found that he could get them so,
  And get them pretty well, he didn't care
So much if he, some evenings, couldn't go,
  But one or other of the two was there,
At every lesson of the course; and though
  Not reckoned as " a couple," were a pair,
Who made the most of opportunities
Which, being his, were hers, or hers, were his.

XXXVIII.

And thus his disappointment, though it fell
  So heavily at first, and though 'twas still
A turn of fortune which contained the knell
  Of hopes that ne'er returned, and never will,

Was robbed of half its bitterness, as well
  For her as for himself. The wind is ill,
They say, that blows nobody any good,
And they were satisfied as matters stood.

XXXIX.

But now the case was sadder far than then;
  He couldn't go to school a season through,
By slyly slipping out and in again,
  Without the knowledge of his father, who,
Among the kindest and the best of men,
  In his stern way, was rather apt to do
Whate'er his judgment held as being best,
And leave to providential care the rest.

XL.

And Will at length began to realize
  That he was destined now to be defeated;—
Of what appeared the fondest earthly prize,
  By force of circumstances to be cheated;
Unless he could contrive some way to rise
  Above impediments, which should be treated
As slight obstructions in his onward way,
To be removed or to be held at bay.

XLI.

He tried all summer, though he tried in vain,
  To get permission that he might arrange
To go to school. He managed to obtain
  Some text books, purchased with a little change
He'd somehow got together, and would fain
  Invest in sciences yet new and strange,
And these he studied nights and Sundays then,
And when at work, went over them again.

XLII.

He thus kept nearly up with one or two
    Acquaintances who were at school, until
His time was out, that is, till he was through
    With what he was expected to fulfil
Of the agreement binding him to do
    A half year's work. The village school had still
Six weeks to run, and then he said, " I know
That Father can't help saying I may go."

XLIII.

But this was also a delusive hope,
    Which, like the rest, would soon be on the wing,
For Mr. Hayden thought, as said by Pope,
    " A little learning is a dangerous thing; "
Nor would he have him give his talents scope,
    By " drinking deep " at the " Pierian spring — "
Or at the spring of scientific lore,
So answered no, as he had done before.

XLIV.

Will's heart sank down within him. He could see
    His cherished purpose was to be resisted
With counter purposes, which seemed to be
    No less determined, and to be insisted
Upon as principles; which somehow he,
    The father, entertained; and there existed
Some instances, 'tis true, where education
Had done some harm without much compensation.

XLV.

I say not Willoughby was angry, yet
    To him his father's course seemed quite unjust,
'Twas not a state of things from which to get
    Much consolation, but to which he must

Submit; and though it did no good to fret,
   He wept by turns, and anxiously discussed
The problem now so difficult to solve,
But came at length to quite a bold resolve.

XLVI.

His dancing school companions, friendly still,
   Had relatives some distance southward, near
A pleasant village where there was a mill,
   And where they used to visit once a year;
And when they had returned, they'd always fill
   His ears with stories, which he loved to hear,
Of what they'd seen and heard, and chanced to do,
Which made him wish that he could go there too.

XLVII.

And then it being farther south, he deemed
   That there the piercing and the bitter cold,
With which the northern winters always teemed,
   At least might partially release its hold.
'Twas painted yellow on the map, and seemed
   As if 'twere fashioned in a milder mold;
Where brighter sunshine gilded wood and lea —
Such dreams as may have come to you or me.

XLVIII.

At least they frequently have come to me,
   Some fairy landscape 'neath a distant sky,
Which I have felt a strong desire to see,
   And sometimes have pursued, scarce knowing why;
Nor have they always proved in fact, to be
   Mere jack-a-lanterns, *ignes fatui*,
Or things imaginary; but indeed,
Some Eldorado to supply my need.

XLIX.

Will told his father he could see no use
   In going longer to the common school;
And therefore he would now propose a truce
   To that, as being nothing but to "fool
Away his time," though this was but a ruse,
   By which to cast his fortunes in the pool
Of chance and circumstance, which might, he thought,
Contain what now the district school could not.

L.

He further said, "If I can go this fall,
   Where Frank has been, and work in that big mill,
At something I can do, I'll send you all,
   Or nearly all I earn; and stay until
It's time to go to work in spring; and call
   It even for the winter, when I will,
Of course come back, if you should want me to,
Or stay, perhaps, and work the whole year through."

LI.

To this the father didn't much object,
   Though this result, that he might not succeed,
Was one, he said, which they must half expect,
   But then he'd see the world, and see the need,
Perhaps, of saving what he could collect
   Of this world's goods; and so it was agreed
That he should try it when his clothes were made,
By some skilled woman of the clothing trade.

LII.

He'd worked a fortnight since his time was out,
   And had four dollars, which he said he guessed
Would pay expenses, or would be about
   Enough, and he could somehow earn the rest,

What he should need, although he had no doubt
    He'd get the job of which he was in quest;
Yet being urged, he took the dollar which
His father offered him, and felt quite rich.

LIII.

His mother's purse was nearly empty; she,
    However, went and took from it the one,
And only coin therein, which chanced to be
    A "fourpence," smoothly worn from service done,
Which giving him, she said, "You'll think of me,
    When this is all that you have left, my son;
'Twill buy some crackers for you then, my dear —"
And on his neck she shed the parting tear.

LIV.

"Be good," she said, "above all things be good,
    Remember Him who gave his life for you,
Who made the sacrifice none other could,
    To save us from our sins. Do not pursue
The vain things of the world, though others should
    Entice you to them; but be ever true
And faithful to the service of the Lord,
That you may gain the Christian's sure reward."

LV.

A mother's love! of all the wondrous things
    This wondrous world exhibits, this is one
Most truly wonderful; which fondly brings
    Its blessing for the deeds of virtue done
Not only, but which also kindly flings
    Its mantle over those that we should shun:
All unsurpassed by aught unless it be
The love of God, vouchsafed to you and me.

LVI.

Will started off when he had thus been dressed,
  By art of tailoress and devotee
Of old St. Crispin, and had been caressed
  By youthful friends whom he had been to see,
Been fondly kissed by sisters, and been blest
  By father and by mother, which to be,
Is happiness that many a youth has known,
But which, in after years, he finds has flown.

LVII.

George carried him as far as he could well
  Drive out and back before it should be night,
And while they rode along, essayed to tell
  What he must do to "get along all right;"
Assuring him that if misfortune fell
  Upon him, he would do whate'er he might,
To help him; and at length he set him down,
Some twenty miles beyond his native town.

LVIII.

His train of thought assumed a sober theme,
  As looking backward with a solemn face,
He mutely stood till George had turned the team,
  Like lover waiting for a last embrace,
And loth to go; nor could he make it seem
  That things were real which were taking place,
As either looked into the other's eye,
And clasping hands, they fondly said good-by.

LIX.

They parted thus, and George returned alone,
  And Will went forward to his destiny;
Which now was partially within his own
  Control, he thought, as he was partly free:

And with a buoyancy he'd seldom known,
   He gazed about, on meadow, hill and tree,
Which 'twas a constant pleasure to behold,
Now dressed in robes of scarlet and of gold.

LX.

He walked a dozen miles that afternoon,
   Until he reached a thrifty railroad town —
The road just being built — and very soon
   Was quartered at an inn of much renown;
And in his room, before the rising moon
   Was fairly up, he wearily sat down,
Before a window, there to feast his eye,
On his imaginary southern sky.

LXI.

At early dawn he went and paid his bill,
   Which so impressed him with its magnitude —
As I have noticed that it often will
   A youthful traveller, a little crude —
That, only for a lodging, as he still
   Had food he brought from home, it seemed, as viewed
By him, extravagant, if not unjust;
As an expensive item which he must,

LXII.

In some way, lessen in the next locality
   Where he should stop, although he scarce knew how,
Or how to ask for private hospitality,
   Among the strangers who would greet him now.
His dreams began to seem like stern reality;
   Yet in his purpose he would not allow
Himself to waver or to hesitate,
But rather, steadily pursued his fate.

LXIII.

Before the evening of the second day,
  He reachèd a village of the smaller size —
Among the many which so calmly lay
  Between the green hills towering to the skies —
One side of which a long pond stretched away,
  And held a floating bridge that used to rise
And fall as did the tide, whose ceaseless flow
Then carried two trip-hammers just below.

LXIV.

And here he stopped a little, hiring out,
  As boy assistant to a carpenter,
For half a month, although he was in doubt
  If he should thus be able to confer
As much as he received, which was about
  The same as ordinary wages were,
For unskilled labor, which at best commands
But poor reward for toil of human hands.

LXV.

The Sunday after his arrival here,
  Attending morning service at the church,
And in the afternoon, it being clear,
  Of out-door pleasures having been in search,
Again at evening, lest he should appear,
  His duty in religious things, to lurch,
He went into the meeting held for prayer;
And as it chanced the parson wasn't there,

LXVI.

The senior deacon took the lead, a lean,
  Old man who had a leg of cork or wood;
Who read the hymns by the uncertain sheen,
  A tallow candle gave, as best he could;

His voice was strong, his intellect was keen,
   His eyesight too, apparently was good,
As aided by the glasses that he wore,
   But that lame leg of his, somehow, before

LXVII.

He brought his reading to the formal close,
   Slipped out of place, and played him false indeed;
Such treatment as we may expect from those
   Who promise largely when there is no need
For friendly offices. His hands arose,
   As by their own volition, to impede
The progress of his fall, in such a plight,
Or to prevent it if perchance he might.

LXVIII.

And throwing up his arms, he threw away,
   Involuntarily, from either hand,
Whatever it contained; that is to say,
   The book from one, which he could not command,
And like a rocket Independence day,
   The candle from the other; which was fanned
By upward flight, some little distance, when,
Like falling meteor, it fell again.

LXIX.

And in its downward path there chanced to sit,
   A fair young maiden, then at "sweet sixteen."
Perhaps her beauty had attracted it,
   Although to say it had I do not mean,
But that some ruffles which she wore were lit,
   As sparks might light a powder magazine;
And quicker far than I can find the phrase
Wherein to tell it, they were all ablaze.

LXX.

And in an instant more, Will Hayden, who
    Was sitting at the time not far away,
Sprang on his feet and quickly darted through
    The little intervening space that lay
Between them; and he knew just what to do,
    For George — in his advice which, on the day
He brought him from his home, he gave to serve
His future needs — had happened to observe,

LXXI.

" Suppose the fire in that great pile of tow,
    Had not been smothered quicker'n lightnin'; then
We'd had the house afire; and don't you know —
    Although we might have gathered all the men
In all creation, and might had 'em throw
    The water from the well or brook — that ten
To one they'd lost it? What then should be done?
Put out your fire before it gets begun."

LXXII.

And on this sage advice Will acted now;
    He threw his arms around her, breast to breast,
In such a manner as should not allow
    A draft of air between them; and he pressed
So firmly that she was compelled to bow
    In mute submission to the strange behest
Of fate — which never could have been foretold —
Until he cautiously released his hold.

LXXIII.

The fire was thus extinguished, but the dress
    Which Mabel wore — for so they christened her —
While feeding it, was injured more or less,
    As is but natural we should infer;

And whether, in the light of his success,
  To thank him for the service or demur
Against the method used, she hardly knew,
And while she hesitated, he withdrew.

LXXIV.

She wasn't able yet to justly prize
  The value of his deed; nor did she know,
At least she didn't fully realize,
  The danger which she had escaped, although
His kindness soon she sought to recognize,
  And much regretted he was gone; and so
There might be, as there often would, no doubt,
Two fires enkindled by the one put out.

LXXV.

At any rate, the following day she wrote
  A line to him, as kindly as could be,
Although I will not undertake to quote
  Therefrom, as that might seem a little free
With private correspondence, but the note
  Expressed an earnest wish that she might see
The one who saved her life, or saved at least,
From greater danger, had the flames increased.

LXXVI.

Her mother too — or rather 'twas her aunt,
  But all the mother she had known of late,
As death, some years before, so grim and gaunt,
  By sad permission of relentless fate,
Had called her mother, and as mortals can't
  Resist the summons, but must all await
Its coming, so did she, and when it came,
She bade it welcome in the Father's name.

LXXVII.

Her aunt, with whom she lived, requested her
   To also say that she'd be very glad
To see him at the house, and to confer
   Some little favor on him, if she had
The opportunity. A wanderer,
   Away from home, he might be feeling sad,
She said, and lonely, and in need of friends —
And who does not need all that heaven sends?

LXXIII.

Will got the note and read it, and replied
   In person, ringing at the cottage door
Where Mabel lived, and while he waited, tried
   To fortify himself by thinking o'er
What might be best to say; and how to hide
   The feeling which had grown to something more
Than he expected, or designed it should,
And when the door was opened, Mabel stood

LXXIX.

Therein, and he was rather at a loss
   To know just what to say or what to do;
The rubicon he was about to cross,
   Demanded courage in a youngster who
Had known but little of the silken floss
   With which the web of love is woven through,
Nor did he much expect, or now intend,
To get in love with her, his new found friend.

LXXX.

He bowed and said, "I got a line from you."
   Said she, "I think you're Mr. Hayden, sir;
And feeling that my hearty thanks were due
   For what you —" here he interrupted her,

And said he came most gladly to renew
   The "short acquaintance" which it might occur
To her, was rather too informal, though
Necessity alone had made it so.

LXXXI.

Extending him her hand, she said again,
   "I thank you kindly for the timely aid
You rendered, though I didn't do it then.
   I should, however, if you'd only staid
A little longer than you did, and when
   My fright was partly over, would have paid
The debt of gratitude which seems so fit,
Or at the least would have acknowledged it."

LXXXII.

She had a blue eye, tranquil and serene,
   From which he saw a pearly tear-drop start;
Her manner seemed a sort of cross between
   A child's simplicity and woman's art
Of gracefulness; and now it could be seen,
   That what she said was from a grateful heart.
She led him in and introduced her aunt,
And mother by adoption, Mrs. Grant.

LXXXIII.

The aunt received him in a kindly way —
   And she was given much to kindly ways,
As all her friends had known for many a day,
   And Mabel knew her as above all praise.
And she of course had something more to say,
   Expressing gratitude in fitting phrase,
For what he had accomplished for "the child,"
As still she called her, and she sweetly smiled

LXXXIV.

Upon him till his heart was captivated
  (A thing which might have chanced to you or me),
As also had been, so 'twas intimated,
  The heart of one much older than was he.
She was a widow, as may be related
  With strict propriety, for aught I see,
As also that, by current information,
A second marriage was in contemplation.

LXXXV.

Howe'er that might have been, she treated Will
  Most kindly; asked if he designed to stay
In town all winter, which appeared to chill
  His spirits some, for he must go away;
Although he hadn't cared for that until
  About this time; and there was naught to say,
Except that he expected soon to go
Some little distance farther " down below."

LXXXVI.

He stayed, however, towards a month in all,
  Till his employer's building was completed;
And once or twice a week he made a call
  At Mrs. Grant's, where he was fondly greeted;
And as the number of the days grew small,
  That he should stay, more frequently repeated
The grateful visits, till the night before
His last look at their hospitable door.

LXXXVII.

Most couples would have been o'er head and ears
  In love by this time, but these two were not;
At least it wasn't spoken, save in tears,
  And words of kindness, speaking true love's thought;

For they remembered they were young in years,
That love with much uncertainty is fraught,
So plighted not their vows as lovers do,
But promised friendship, loving, just and true.

LXXXVIII.

The morning after they had said good-by.
    Expressing each to each their strong good-will,
He took his satchel — not without a sigh —
    And so resumed his journey to the mill,
Where he designed to work; at least to try
    To get a situation he could fill,
But now he wished he might continue where
He had been, for his heart must still be there.

LXXXIX.

Then he remembered what his brother said,
    " Don't get in love before you're twenty-one,"
Among the rules by which he would be led,
    To some extent, all dangerous roads to shun ;
And this especially ran through his head,
    " Put out your fire before it gets begun ; "
But now it had begun, and yet he tried
To put it out, or from himself to hide

XC.

Its burning ; though it still kept smouldering low,
    While he was trying to extinguish it,
Nor did he any cogent reason know,
    Why its continuance be deemed unfit,
Except that he was young, and meant to go
    To school, perhaps some years before he quit —
And thus he plodded o'er life's onward track,
Half looking forward and half looking back.

XCI.

As many a man has done, in vain regret,
    For some misfortune or mistake or sin;
Or in remembrance of some joy, which yet
    Lights up the path he still is walking in;
Or in the hope that ere his sun shall set,
    Some good thing yet may be which might have been:
Thus living in the past and future, more
Than in the present, which we oft ignore.

XCII.

The turnpike over which his journey lay,
    Was on a broad, high belt of cultured land,
Which to the valley gently sloped away,
    Though quite unevenly, on either hand,
With hills and mountains still beyond; and they
    Made up a view most picturesque and grand:
One, as it lay beneath the mellow sheen
Of "Indian Summer," worthy to be seen.

XCIII.

Nor was the glamour of his distant view,
    Yet dissipated by the present one,
Which seemed to him not altogether new;
    Which, as it glistened in the autumn sun,
Was painted nearly in the selfsame hue
    That he imagined when he had begun
To build air castles in the neighborhood
Where now he looked on hill and dale and wood.

XCIV.

Why should it be? Those who have ever seen
    The lovely picture which I here essay
To feebly paint, in all its hues of green
    And gold and red, which on his pathway lay,

Or others similar, that lie between
   The Green Hills and the White, when pass away
The summer days, will readily conceive
Them equal to what fancy e'er might weave.

XCV.

The day was one which only autumn sees,
   The golden harvest gathered, blade and ear,
The gorgeous hues upon the maple trees,
   The culminating grandeur of the year.
I've often thought, when I've communed with these,
   An Indian Summer day had not its peer,
For sweet enchantment and for loveliness,
The troubled soul to soothe and calm and bless.

XCVI.

" There was that nameless splendor everywhere "
   (As sang the Cambridge bard in rhythm sweet),
" That wild exhilaration in the air,
   Which makes the passers in the city street "
(And those no less in country places fair)
   " Congratulate each other as they meet ; "
And Will had reason to congratulate
Himself that he was now so fortunate.

XCVII.

Through all that day, so cloudless and serene,
   He journeyed southward at a rapid pace,
Till twenty miles were said to intervene,
   Between his present and his former place ;
And every charming picture he had seen,
   Contained an image of fair Mabel's face,
Which, though 'twas absent, he could not forget —
Could not or would not, or at least not yet.

XCVIII.

The third day brought him to the woollen mill;
   And at the counting-room he asked if they
Had any vacancies they'd like to fill,
   And was surprised to hear the agent say
They'd just discharged some workmen, and had still
   As many left as they could make it pay
To keep at further work; for he, somehow,
Had not allowed himself to look, till now,

XCIX.

Much on the dark side of the picture he
   Had drawn so fondly of his prospects where
It seemed to him he needed but to be,
   To find enjoyable surroundings there.
Now he began reluctantly to see
   That he was building castles in the air;
Or phantom ships, to vanish out of sight,
Like some mirage of evanescent light.

C.

He couldn't bring himself to quite submit
   To such an overthrow of such a plan
As he'd been laying, and abandon it,
   And so he queried further of the man,
As o'er his mind a new hope seemed to flit,
   "I'd like to see the owner if I can,
If you are not the owner;" for he thought,
From what he'd said already, he was not.

CI.

The agent told him rather curtly where
   The owner lived, but said, "You'll throw away
The precious time you spend in going there,
   For Mr. Reed will have no word to say,

Concerning it." But Will thought he could spare
    The time, and so he went without delay,
And told the man his history in brief,
    And how he came from home to get relief,

CII.

From present difficulties; and until
    He could afford to spend a term at school,
He'd like a job of some kind in the mill;
    But Mr. Reed replied that as a rule,
The chances were but few. He said, " I will,
    However — though 'twould be a little cool
And wet — employ you on a second dam
I'm building up the stream from where I am."

CIII.

His wife, who chanced to hear the conversation,
    Approached them, saying it would be too bad,
To think of giving such a situation,
    At that cold season, to so young a lad;
" Let's see," she said, in seeming meditation,
    " Who was that man the other day that had
A district school, for which he tried to get
A teacher? He may not have found one yet.

CIV.

" This boy can teach a little school like that —
    I think 'twas one away up on the hill; —"
Will brightened up and twirled around his hat,
    Which he was holding in his fingers still,
And said he should be highly pleased thereat,
    But feared he wasn't qualified to fill
The high position of a teacher, though
He'd studied some, as he perhaps, could show.

CV.

As Mr. Reed remembered who it was,
  They both encouraged him to go and see
The school committee, right away, because
  'Twas getting late, and possibly might be
Too late already; so without much pause,
  And when the mantle clock had just struck three,
He thanked them for advice so kindly meant,
And started off upon this new intent.

CVI.

The lady asked him to come in again, —
  To leave his satchel, which he gladly did,
Then hurried onward up a narrow glen,
  Where, 'mong the trees, a rapid stream was hid,
Until he'd walked a mile or two, and then,
  As joyous as the scene he walked amid,
Went up a hill into the neighborhood
Where he would turn schoolmaster, if he could.

CVII.

He found the house where lived the school committee,
  Whose name was Jones, and rapped upon the door,
And made his application. "'Tis a pity,"
  Said Mr. Jones, "that you have not had more
Experience; we need a man that's gritty,
  To keep our school, and not get run ashore;
There's two or three stout boys that want to know
Who's master all the time, or out you go.

CVIII.

"How old are you? You can't be at the most,
  Much over twenty, judging by your face —"
And then appeared to Will the weazen ghost
  Of false dissimulation; for in case

He should admit that he could only boast
   Of eighteen years, he'd hardly get the place,
He so much coveted, whereas he might
   If he could pass for twenty, near or quite.

CIX.

"Don't tell a lie unless you're cornered," said
   His brother on the way; and this was not
The kind of corner he had then been led
   To think might be legitimate. He thought
'Twould be a breaking of the rule instead;
   And had besides, some love for truth, which got
The better of his fears, and he replied,
"I'm eighteen only, and eight months beside."

CX.

"Eighteen," said Mr. Jones, "will never do;
   It's far too young, and I shall have to get
Somebody that is older, some one who
   Will not be quite as liable to let
The boys run over him." Thus even through
   His virtues, did the tide of fortune set
Against him seemingly, as oft it will;
But I shall try to keep him virtuous still.

CXI.

His prospects thus had fallen to the ground,
   And all his recent hopes been crushed again.
He sat in sorrow, more or less profound,
   And wondered what 'twere best he should do then.
He presently got up and turned around,
   To get his hat and say good evening, when
Another rap was heard upon the door,
Where stood a stout young man of twenty-four.

CXII.

He too had come to make his application
   For that same school, he having heard that day,
That there was still a vacant situation,
   Which must be filled without much more delay,
As it was late, and on the information
   That Mr. Jones was authorized to say
Who now should fill it, he had come to ask
If he could have the pleasure of the task.

CXIII.

"Well, well," said Mr. Jones, "now here are two
   That want the little school, to be begun
Week after next. I'll tell you what I'll do,
   Between the two I'll take the stoutest one;
Which will determine as to who is who,
   Much more than scholarship, before you're done,
As either knows enough, I have no doubt,
To teach our school, if he could keep it out.

CXIV.

"Now you may wrestle, lift, or what you will,
   To try the cause between you, though I deem
This oldest one best qualified to fill
   The present situation. It may seem
But fair, however, that you try your skill,
   And should this boy be beaten, my esteem
For him would be no less, but in our school,
We need more strength than learning, as a rule."

CXV.

Will looked as if it had surprised him some,
   This novel method of examination
Of fitness for the school curriculum,
   Which should consist of muscular inflation,

And when to such a crisis things had come,
　　He said, "You're under no such obligation
To me, and there's no question which of us
　　Would be selected, if examined thus.

CXVI.

"I therefore such a contest will decline,
　　In favor of my senior and superior;
Although I can but think that your design
　　Of governing by force, will prove inferior
To that which, being teacher, would be mine,
　　That is, of cultivating the interior,
And better nature of the boys that you,
In your selection, seem to have in view."

CXVII.

Which Mr. Jones good naturedly received,
　　But said his confidence in gentle rule,
Was very small indeed; that he believed
　　In rod and ferule in the common school.
"Whate'er in theory may be achieved,"
　　He said, "if you should ever try it, you'll
Discover that it don't succeed, I fear —
At least I shouldn't want to try it here."

CXVIII.

Will said good night, and hurried back to town,
　　Disheartened by the failures of the day;
Although he bore up under fortune's frown
　　As well as I should, I presume to say.
He half regretted that he e'er came down,
　　But still insisted that he'd come to stay,
Whene'er he found himself debating whether
To now give up his purpose altogether.

CXIX.

It being late, he went into the inn,
    And asked the landlord what his charges were,
For meals and lodging; told him where he'd been,
    That he was now a sort of wanderer,
In search of work. "I've been through thick and thin,"
    The host replied, "till I can hardly stir;
My boy's been sick, and now he isn't well,
If you'll take hold, I'll hire you for a spell."

CXX.

Will said he would accept, with due respect,
    And after supper, went and milked the cow,
And did whate'er the other might direct;
    Went up and got his bag, and told them how
He'd been examined, not in intellect,
    But on his muscle, as a teacher, "Now,"
He said, "I'll wait another year, and then,
To get a winter school will try again."

CXXI.

He was a man of all work, so to speak,
    As those in such positions always are;
Had seven days to labor in the week,
    To fetch and carry, whether near or far;
Kept up the fires, for then 'twas cold and bleak,
    And not infrequently he tended bar;
Sold brandy, rum and gin to all who came,
Although he did it in another's name.

CXXII.

And yet he found some little time to read,
    And some to play old sledge and euchre, though
An innovation on his simple creed,
    In playing games, had somehow seemed to grow

In favor with the boys whom now, indeed,
    He was compelled to play with, or forego
His playing altogether, as he should,
    But compromised with evil and with good.

CXXIII.

As many do in this, our mundane sphere,
    By doing good and evil deeds by turns;
Or partly doing what it seems quite clear
    Should be excluded from the world's concerns;
Resisting much, with purposes sincere,
    Although the moral lamp so feebly burns,
And sheds its light with such a flickering sheen,
As not, at times, to be distinctly seen.

CXXIV.

"Don't ever gamble," was a rule laid down
    By George, when coming, as they rode along,
"No sooner for a penny than a crown,
    Because the principle is wholly wrong.
Although solicited by king or clown,
    The evil influence however strong,
Don't ever do it, as none ever should."
And Will responded that he never would.

CXXV.

A promise isn't much, and yet it may
    Just turn the scale 'twixt purpose and desire;
And in a bitter conflict keep at bay,
    The beast of passion, with his eyes of fire:
The ghost of sore temptation help to lay,
    And chant its requiem on the golden lyre
Of virtue in its triumph, largely due
To honest pledges to be just and true.

CXXVI.

One night when Will had worked about a week,
  He being in the bar-room down below,
A German barber, who had learned to speak
  The English language with a ready flow,
And knew as much of cribbage, whist, bezique,
  And other games, as most young fellows know —
Whose shop another basement room was in —
Approached the bar and asked him for some gin.

CXXVII.

There also sat beneath the chandelier,
  At least beneath the single lamp, which hung
Above a table standing pretty near
  The corner of the bar, whereon it flung
Its dazzling rays in token of good cheer,
  And shed its light of varied hues among
The bottles and decanters standing there,
Three more young fellows, who should all beware.

CXXVIII.

One was a farmer's son who often came
  Into the village on a lowery day,
And, rather careless of his own good name,
  He would at times, indulge in drink and play;
Although he hadn't learned each "little game,"
  By which the sharpers often get away
With simple folk, so foolish as to try
What they are pretty sure of losing by.

CXXIX.

Another was a clerk, who'd just come in
  From his employer's store; who boarded there;
The other played upon the violin,
  At dancing parties, where the young and fair

So oft indulge in this peculiar sin,
  If 'tis a sin, as many would declare,
Though I will not ; but think perhaps it might
Be held as harmless if conducted right.

CXXX.

The barber said, " Come boys, let's take a drink ; "
  And thereupon the others gathered round.
" Take what you like." The fiddler said, " I think
  I'll take some brandy." After some profound
Reflection, which might well have made him shrink
  From treading farther on such dangerous ground,
The clerk said, " I will take some beer I guess."
As did the farmer, for its harmlessness,

CXXXI.

O thou, King Alcohol! thy legions slay
  Their many thousand victims every year ;
Approaching in such surreptitious way
  As least alarms them, with thy wine and beer.
Oh, would some moral giant come and lay
  Thee low forever; for I deem thy peer,
In deeds of wickedness, could not again
Be found to decimate the ranks of men.

CXXXII.

The barber said again, " Had we some cards,
  I'd now propose a game of poker, though
My pile is not as big as old Girard's,
  And you are sharpers, as I chance to know ;
Yet with a recklessness which disregards
  All consequences, if for weal or woe,
I feel as if I'd like to try a hand,
Of course for pleasure, as you understand."

CXXXIII.

They got the cards, and they were white and clean,
   They staked some money to make up "the pool,"
And while they sought each other's wealth to glean,
   Will sat philosophizing on his stool.
'Twas such a sight as he had never seen,
   The education of a novel school;
Which he, however, by his pledge, had been
Prohibited from taking lessons in.

CXXXIV.

He thought of what his father always taught,
   That playing cards led straight to gambling; yet
His brother George, who played, had only sought
   To so impress him that he shouldn't bet;
And he had promised, as he clearly ought,
   To never do it, but to firmly set
His face against it, as he thought he'd done,
But found the task was scarcely yet begun.

CXXXV.

The barber dealt, and managed, unobserved,
   To deal himself six cards instead of five;
And then withdrawing one from those which served
   For present use — that future hands might thrive —
And with design from which he never swerved,
   He put it in his sleeve, to so contrive
To keep it from the other players' ken,
Until the next in turn should deal again.

CXXXVI.

And when the others dealt, of course he would
   Again have six, from which he might select,
By changing them about, as best he could —
   When they would not be likely to detect

The movement — so to keep his number good,
    By methods not considered quite correct,
By honest players of an honest game;
Which would on him have brought no little blame,

CXXXVII.

If they had been discovered, like the play
    The Heathen Chinee made with William Nye;
But as it was, the others couldn't say
    That he had not played honestly; and why
He often held much better hands than they,
    They only could conjecture. By and by,
The farmer's boy, however, grew suspicious,
And went away, more wise and less ambitious,

CXXXVIII.

In that direction; and with less of cash,
    And reputation, than he had before.
'Tis true that "he that steals my purse, steals trash,"
    But these young men had stolen something more
From one another; and he now would "dash
    The wine cup down," and solemnly he swore
He'd never bet again; a virtuous vow,
Which he, for aught I know, has kept till now.

CXXXIX.

When he was gone, the barber turned and said,
    "Perhaps this new bar tender here would play;"
But Will, when thus invited, shook his head,
    And said he didn't know the game which they
Were playing then, he'd played old sledge instead,
    Although he'd played but little any way,
And wouldn't play for money if he could,
As he had promised that he never would.

CXL.

"That's well enough," the barber said, "and yet
   All games would lose their interest for me,
If playing them, I didn't lose or get
   Some money out of it, as there would be
No such excitement as a little bet
   Affords the player, just enough to see
If fortune favors him, or 'see' perchance,
The hand some one has bet on in advance."

CXLI.

And then, continuing, he said, "If this
   Young man will play, I'll tell you what I'll do,
I'll take him for a partner, hit or miss,
   And play old sledge for just a game or two;"
As if he would betray him with a kiss,
   Which many a worthy youth has fallen through,
Since Jesus was betrayed in that same way,
And many more, perhaps, before his day.

CXLII.

Will still replied he couldn't play for stakes;
"You needn't," said the other, "I will stand
   For both, and lose or win what our side makes
Or loses, while you help me play the hand.
I'll risk you; we ourselves are no great shakes,
   At any game;" and with a smile so bland,
And words so soft, he o'erpersuaded him,
Although the argument was pretty slim.

CXLIII.

Will went around and took the vacant chair
   The farmer boy had sat in; and they played
For twenty cents a game, each player's share
   Thus being five, which on the board was laid,

The barber having twice the interest there,
  The others had, while Will no wager made;
But played his hand as wisely as he could,
His partner saying it was very good.

CXLIV.

At any rate, when they had played a spell,
  And had decided it was time to quit,
The barber's wallet had been made to swell,
  By further winnings being put in it;
Though not so much, perhaps, that Will played well,
  As by his own superior talent, wit,
Or skill or knowledge, enterprise, or what
You please, whereby he carried out his plot.

CXLV.

The game was finished, but the party sat
  Around the table for a little yet,
Though hardly in a mood for friendly chat,
  As each was entertaining some regret,
Except the barber; and as being pat
  To such occasion, and in hopes to set
The tide of feeling in the right direction,
He sang the following song for their reflection.

BRIER AND THORN.*

Should fortune sometimes coldly smile,
  Should fate defeat some fond design,
Should hope deceive, or love beguile,
  Or friends desert, or foes malign:
Remember sorrow comes to all,
  To disappointment all are born,
Some grief may every joy forestall,
  As every rose has brier and thorn.

* See sheet music by publishers of book, in the absence of which, sing in Bonny Doon.

Should best endeavors be in vain,
  Should prospects fail which seemed so fair,
Should pleasure only purchase pain,
  Or find some deeply hidden snare;
Should chance and circumstance conspire
  To render highest hopes forlorn,
Remember still the thorn and brier,
  That every rose has brier and thorn.

But, though misfortunes darkly lower,
  Although the sky be overcast,
Although there's many a cheerless hour,
  The happier days may come at last;
However dark the night may be,
  At length awakes the brightening morn,
When hearts may be from sorrow free,
  The rose be free from brier and thorn.

CXLVI.

The clerk and fiddler gone, the barber stepped
  Before the bar, and on the counter laid
A dollar bill, which Will would please accept,
  In compensation for his timely aid.
He hesitated some before he kept
  The money thus for such a service paid,
But finally he yielded to the whim,
By which the other had rewarded him.

CXLVII.

The barber said good night and walked away;
  Will closed the bar and went up-stairs to bed;
"Don't ever gamble," he could hear George say,
  "I never will," kept running through his head:
His mother taught him every night to pray,
  Which he neglected now, although he said,
At least said mentally, before he slept,
"I thank kind Heaven for the promise kept."

CXLVIII.

O grace! thou savest by a single hair,
    Sometimes from actual and deadly sin;
And many a saint has just escaped the snare
    That many a sinner has been taken in;
Or may have had, at least, not much to spare,
    Between what was and that which might have been,
And Will had little when he thus had played,
And such a nice discrimination made.

CXLIX.

So Job escaped one time, you recollect,
    From sore affliction, and from underneath
The hand of death, when he could scarce expect
    To see the sword returning to its sheath;
When all the margin which he could detect,
    Was just the outer membrane on his teeth;
A margin which — to Will's somewhat akin —
May be regarded as a little thin.

CL.

A few days afterwards, there came again,
    An opportunity for Will to play,
With this same barber and two other men,
    Which he consented to; that is to say,
His partner took the chances, now as then,
    And got the best of them, and got away
With several dollars, by some indirection,
Which still he practised, and without detection.

CLI.

And when the game was done, he gave to Will,
    A small percentage, as he had before,
Of that which he had gained; and sought to fill
    His heart with love of such peculiar lore

As gamblers use. "You've played quite well, but still,"
   He smiling said, "there may be something more,
That I could tell you if you cared to know,
Although for now, perhaps we'll let it go."

CLII.

Thus matters ran along a month or two,
   Will drifting slowly downward in the tide;
Though he to all his pledges yet was true,
   Grim vice and virtue running side by side,
As they have often done with people who
   Have loved the one while they have feebly tried
To cultivate the other more or less,
By deeds of charity or righteousness.

CLIII.

He didn't seem to fully realize
   That he was letting down his moral tone,
Though that could scarcely have been otherwise,
   With common vices so familiar grown,
With none to cheer, admonish or advise,
   No arm to lean upon except his own,
And so surrounded as he had been here,
By such a murky moral atmosphere.

CLIV.

Just after New Year's, of an afternoon,
   As Will was studying, a leisure hour —
For still he coveted the precious boon
   Of education, with its magic power,
And like a lover gazing at the moon,
   Behind the lattice of a lady's bower,
He dreamed of happiness which by and by,
He should enjoy beneath a cloudless sky —

CLV.

He heard somebody coming through the door;
    And when he looked around, who should it be
But Mr. Jones, whom he had known before,
    The school committee whom he went to see?
And who, approaching him, remarked, "'Twas more
    To run that school than my man thought for: he
Began with no misgivings, fear or doubt,
But only yesterday they put him out.

CLVI.

"And I've come down," he then went on to say,
    "To see if you would like to go and try
To keep it out by your peculiar way
    Of governing by kindness now, though I
Have little confidence in such boys' play,
    But something must be done, and by and by —
Yes, right away, if you should not succeed,
I'll get a sheriff, which is what they need.

CLVII.

"There's one good thing," continued he, "with you,
    You seem to like your studies pretty well,
I guess you never mingle with the crew
    My boy saw round that table there a spell
Ago, for they were gambling, as he knew,
    Although he didn't know, or didn't tell,
Just who they were, except the barber here,
And he was cheating like a modern seer."

CLVIII.

Will wasn't flattered, but chagrined by this,
    He felt rebuked not only, but he saw
Some little likelihood that he might miss
    His opportunity, through that same flaw

Of reputation ; and the deep abyss,
  Which he'd been standing over, yet might draw
Him in, and Mr. Jones perhaps might find
What he had really done, and change his mind.

CLIX.

He said, however, that he would accept
  The situation, if they could agree,
Provided Mr. Redington, who kept
  The house, could spare him ; and he'd go and see:
But first he hurriedly and slyly crept
  Up stairs and packed his things, that he might be
All ready when he got permission, so
As not to leave the landlord down below,

CLX.

With Mr. Jones, for fear there might be done,
  Some mischief with the tongue ; which would have been
No new phenomenon beneath the sun,
  As that is not the most uncommon sin
That plagues humanity ; which every one
  Has neighbors who are oft indulging in,
To speak of others' failings now and then —
And they are common with the best of men.

CLXI.

He then found Mr. Redington, who made
  Upon his services no further claim;
"In fact," he said, "already you have stayed
  Beyond what I expected when you came,"
And what he owed him, he went in and paid,
  And he and Mrs. R., a genial dame,
Expressed the wish that he might prosper still,
And Mr. Jones and he rode up the hill.

CLXII.

"And now," said Mrs. Jones, "you've got the boy,"
   On seeing them come in, "perhaps he can,
Some boyish or some cunning arts employ,
   That wouldn't suit so well an older man;
I'm sure," she said to him, "we shall enjoy
   Your being here, I wished when school began,
Or pretty soon at least, we'd taken you —
Here's my boy Fred, I know he's good and true."

CLXIII.

When introduced to Mrs. Jones's son,
   Will thought the latter turned a little pale,
As he himself quite likely would have done,
   With change of circumstances in the tale
That hung thereby. He knew him as the one
   Who came into the bar room, drank the ale,
And played at poker several weeks before,
Whose seat he took when Fred would play no more.

CLXIV.

And now the new schoolmaster, as he thought,
   Might not, perhaps, regard him as an equal,
But an inferior, who should be taught,
   And taught that dissipation has a sequel;
Especially when he was fairly caught,
   By one who knew his habits didn't speak well
For former training, and for education
In ways too common in the Yankee nation.

CLXV.

Said Will, "I think I've seen your face before."
   The other nothing said, but looked his answer;
Which was, "For heaven's sake say nothing more,"
   For memory stung him like a moral cancer.

He felt uncertain if he'd best implore
  His secrecy, or say, "I'm not the man, sir,
You're quite mistaken," if he should suggest
The circumstances, but was set at rest,

CLXVI.

By Will's observing in a kindly way,
  "'Twas in the bar room if I recollect,
Some time ago; and now I trust we may,
  As time goes on, be friends; and I expect
To need some kind assistance, as they say
  That several boys who voted to reject
My predecessor's further teaching, will,
Quite likely, make the same objection still."

CLXVII.

The mother answered for the boy again,
  " He'll help you what he can to keep 'em steady,
He'll be a sort of spy, and tell you when
  There's trouble coming, so you may be ready; —
But we'll have supper now, here come the men,
  From chopping wood; sit down right there by Freddie,
He'll wait upon you if I shouldn't think
To give you what you want to eat or drink."

CLXVIII.

When grace was said, as common Christian use is,
  Or was with Mr. Jones, his wife declared
That she should not attempt to make excuses
  About her supper, though it was prepared
A little hastily. And where the deuce is
  The sense in telling people who have shared
Your hospitality, that tisn't good?
Which Mrs. Jones at least, scarce ever would.

CLXIX.

She said, in fact, she fancied she could cook,
　About as well as any of them did,
When, having time, she really undertook
　To thus exhibit what her pantry hid:
She also could, by word or act or look,
　While granting some, some other things forbid;
As now, although her food was good and ample,
She had one thing she meant they shouldn't sample.

CLXX.

She asked her husband if he'd have some pie;
　Though she remarked that it was rather new,
And not as good as 'twould be by and by,
　"Not any? no? nor you? nor you? nor you?"
She said, as, holding it up pretty high,
　She moved it towards each one, and quickly drew
It back, before they could have answered no
Or yes.　"Then I won't cut it; let it go."

CLXXI.

She thought she'd like to save it, and besides,
　She loved the " cunning arts " which she suggested
That Will might use if evil should betide,
　Or from his grasp the sceptre should be wrested;
Or thus avert the evil, thus to guide
　The sceptred hand and sway, still unmolested;
As she appeared to do in her affairs,
Her household being governed unawares.

CLXXII.

Not strictly honest, she was very good;
　Like some that I have seen; and *vice versa,*
I've known an honest man who never could
Be found at any deed of love or mercy;

Although to principle he firmly stood,
  Unchanging as the stars in Major Ursa; —
And some, not very good have seemed to me,
Nor honest either to a high degree.

CLXXIII.

That night, it being time to go to bed,
  As Mrs. Jones suggested, Fred and Will
Went up together, for he roomed with Fred,
  Up in the parlor chamber, cold and still.
" I'll come and take the light away," she said,
  " And tuck you up," as so she did, until
She'd got them fixed as nicely as she might,
And then she kissed them both and said good night.

CLXXIV.

'And Fred inquired, " Do you remember when
  You saw me in the bar room?" — " Yes, I do;"
And he continued, " Well, I swore off then,
  From playing poker and from drinking, too."
" That's right," said Will, " don't ever play again,
  Or drink with any one, no matter who."
Fred said he wouldn't, " but I hope," said he,
" You'll never tell them what you know of me.

CLXXV.

" And you may know, perhaps, as I believe,
  The barber cheated us like thunderation;
And stole the cards, and stuck 'em in his sleeve;
  At least I thought so from my observation:
My father asked me if I could conceive
  Of honest gambling, when, in explanation
Of where I was, I told him I went in
And saw them play, and saw the barber win."

CLXXVI.

Will said he didn't know, but shouldn't be
    At all surprised to learn that it was so;
"But then," he said, "he never cheated me,
    And that is something I am glad to know"
(A show of virtue which we often see),
    "Nor will he you again unless you go
Where he can get a chance, which now you say
You never will; I trust you never may."

CLXXVII.

Said Mr. Jones, next morning, "Have you got
    No rule, no preparation for a fight?"
"I have no rule," said Willoughby, "I thought
    If they were bound to put me out, they might;
Which they, of course, can do as well as not,
    Unless I make them think it isn't right,
Or isn't best for them, as I expect
To do, unless all reason they reject."

CLXXVIII.

Then he and Fred set off, and on the way,
    Fred told him who the "ugly fellows" were,
And he was studying what he could say,
    That should invite no possible demur,
And laying plans for getting through the day,
    And hoping nothing serious might occur,
Until they reached the noisy schoolhouse, where
Fred introduced as many as were there.

CLXXIX.

Will rapped his fingers lightly on the table,
    And said 'twas time to then begin the school,
And made such wise remarks as he was able,
    "I come," he said, "with neither rod nor rule;

A government by force is too unstable;" —
One whispered to another, "He's a fool,
To think in this school he can govern so,
Let's lick him." "Lick him?" said the other, "no;

CLXXX.

"We'd all be fools to lick a master who
    Has no conveniences for lickin' us;
If that's the way the fellow's goin' to do,
    I'll never try to make a bit of fuss;
And by the great horn spoon, I'll help him too,
    If ever he should get into a muss,
I tell you that's the kind of folks I like,
And I propose that we stand by him, Ike."

CLXXXI.

Thus having told them what they might expect,
    He mildly said, "we'll now make up our classes;"
And they were ready, as he might direct,
    And with a willingness that far surpasses
All forced endeavor of the intellect,
    In gaining knowledge which the mind amasses,
They went to their legitimate vocation,
With no design of insubordination.

CLXXXII.

How well the teacher had been qualified,
    For such a task as he had undertaken,
By way of scholarship, may be implied;
    His own self-confidence was not unshaken,
Although at present he had only tried,
    Their moral sensibilities to waken;
Yet his attainments had been something more
Than A B C in scientific lore.

CLXXXIII.

His grammar was at least as good as that
   We see on tombstones, signs and railway stations;
And in the cars, I often marvel at
   The wondrous learning of the corporations;
Or those who manage them, who may have sat
   In legislative halls of states or nations;
But haven't wit enough in many cases,
To put their commas in their proper places.

CLXXXIV.

And memory suggests an instance, where
   A leading road has made a handsome show
Of station buildings. Should you happen there,
   And have the curiosity to know
How learned they are, and have the time to spare,
   Go on the platform, where the others go,
And you will see, as tidy as a broom,
The stylish entrance to the "Ladie's Room."

CLXXXV.

At one state capital, if you should still
   Have further leisure to investigate,
And it should happen, as it often will,
   That in the ladies' room you chance to wait,
You'll see where "Ticket's," with a master's skill,
   Are duly advertised; and I might state
More cases of the kind than you would care
To read, if I had time and space to spare.

CLXXXVI.

There lived a blacksmith, sometime in the past,
   Whose shop was shaded by some maple trees,
Along Mad River, where his lot was cast,
   Whose learning would compare with some of these;

For when the angels came for him at last,
  He left his ledger to his legatees,
Which many balances were still uncrossed in,
And one was duly charged to " olesam osten."

CLXXXVII.

It may be reckoned in a man like me,
  Somewhat ungenerous to criticise
My neighbors' blunderings, when all can see
  That I myself am not extremely wise;
At least not cultured to a high degree,
  But then 'tis customary to advise
Our fellows of their faults, no matter though
Our own be greater, as the world may know.

CLXXXVIII.

But to my story; for I must begin,
  More rapidly to hasten to the end,
Which at the best is still some distance in
  The future of events. If heaven send
Such inspiration as shall serve to win
  The kind approval of each reading friend,
I shall, however, have been richly paid,
For all pains taken and all efforts made.

CLXXXIX.

Will had no trouble with the scholars who,
  When justly treated, could be just in turn;
Or all at least excepting one or two,
  Whose discontent, at first gave some concern,
But they began, before the term was through,
  Ere many days, in fact, began to learn,
That opposition to so mild a rule,
Was not to be encouraged by the school.

CXC.

The term was finished, Will had got his pay,
   And felt quite satisfied, with ample reason;
Was asked to promise, ere he went away,
   That he would not engage another season,
Till Mr. Jones had seen him; which to say,
   He deemed would be a sort of moral treason
Against his liberty, and so he said
He'd see a little later on, instead.

CXCI.

Then light of heart and with a heavy purse,
   That is to say, a heavy one for him,
From which, however, he must soon disburse,
   By sending home, enough to make it slim
Again — than which a thousand things were worse —
   He sought the village, there his sails to trim,
For such fair winds as might perchance arise,
To waft him onward 'neath the summer skies.

CXCII.

In teaching others, he himself was taught,
   Or rather had imbibed some higher notions,
Concerning problems which were never wrought
   Completely out by all the world's devotions,
To science or religion; which have sought,
   By theological and moral potions,
To put the world upon its good behavior;
To find from sin a universal savior.

CXCIII.

And men of ethics have debated whether
   All things were sinful that might lead to sin;
And oft confounded right and wrong together,
   At times apparently somewhat akin;

And left the boundaries of virtue's tether —
Where that should justly end and vice begin —
But ill defined, and sometimes nearly gone;
And these my hero had been studying on.

CXCIV.

That he already had been quite beyond
   The strictest moral bounds, he was aware;
At least in some directions, being fond
   Of that which led him to the evil snare;
Though what was stipulated in the bond
   Of pledge and promise, he had taken care,
If not in spirit, should be kept in form,
A partial shelter from the threatening storm.

CXCV.

He now, however, had made up his mind
   That he would keep it in an honest way,
No matter whether otherwise inclined,
   No matter what somebody else might say;
But oft it happens, when we have designed
   To put away our sins without delay,
And keep them hid, as well as put to rout,
That past offences somehow find us out.

CXCVI.

Will went and saw the Redingtons, and then
   The Mrs. Reed whose husband owned the mill,
And she expressed much satisfaction when
   She heard of his success; but there was still
A query in her looks. She said again,
   "I've heard an ugly thing about you, Will;
The landlord said that, though he liked you well,
You gambled some. Now is it true, pray tell?"

CXCVII.

"No ma'am," said Will, "it isn't true, and yet
    I may have given that impression; I
Have played in games wherein the others bet,
    And laid their money on the board close by;
And those who saw us playing, might have set
    Me down as one of them." "No reason why
They shouldn't," said the other, "but I'm glad
To hear you say it isn't quite as bad

CXCVIII.

As I had heard. How did it happen, though?"
    He told her of the facts, the conversation
Between the barber and himself, to show
    That he declined at each solicitation,
To play for money, as my readers know;
    And Mrs. Reed declared the explanation
Was not unsatisfactory; "but then,"
She said, "don't ever go so far again.

CXCIX.

Don't play with those who gamble any way;
    And this reminds me," still continued she,
"That yesterday I heard my husband say
    He some expected, pretty soon, that he
Should have to get some one to come and stay,
    And help the man that sorts the wool. 'Twould be
A better place for you than 'twould be where
You were before; they're too immoral there.

CC.

And then besides, when you were tending bar,
    'Twas not by any means a safe position,
For one so young; how many men there are
    Who owe their sad and destitute condition

To dissipation; and it isn't far
　From selling drinks to drink; a thin partition
Is that between them, as a rule, I think,
For those that sell, they say most always drink."

CCI.

Will said he had no appetite for rum,
　But used to think, when he was selling it,
When some poor drinking fellow used to come,
　That 'twas a business which was hardly fit
To get a living by, and he had some
　Misgivings then, as well as since he quit;
Nor did he now expect to work again
In such position as he had done then.

CCII.

The Mr. McElroy who sorted wool,
　Was oldish now and wasn't very well,
And he had had a long and steady pull,
　And chronic ailments he could not dispel;
Until his hands were rather more than full,
　With all the duties which upon him fell,
And Mr. Reed had thought it might be best,
A little later, he should have a rest.

CCIII.

And so he offered Will a situation,
　As his assistant, though with moderate pay,
And some assurance that his compensation
　Might be augmented at no distant day;
And in a spirit of accommodation,
　Did Mrs. Reed invite him there to stay,
And make his home with her, until he could
" Procure a better one, or one as good."

CCIV.

Thus Will was quartered in the very mill
    Which his imagination long had gilded,
With golden garnish, such as used to fill
    The fairy castles he so long had builded,
When fancy roamed according to its will,
    As in the past it did, and as it still did;
For now, while he was very well contented,
His old imaginings were supplemented

CCV.

With something yet to be. 'Tis ever thus;
    "Man never is, but always to be blest;"
No matter how kind fortune favors us,
    With that of which we fain would be possessed;
We're ever anxious, always clamorous,
    For something more, of which we are in quest,
And always hoping, till life's sun is set,
That ere its setting we may find it yet.

CCVI.

And this is progress I suppose, and so
    A part of that which nature had designed.
I make small progress with my story, though
    The next succeeding canto we may find —
But that I cannot tell, save as we go,
    And at the present time I feel inclined
To take a rest; and so, perhaps, do you;
May you your reading, I my task, renew.

WILLOUGHBY'S WISDOM.

CANTO FIFTH.

I.

Six summers Will was busy sorting wool,
   An academic student in the fall;
Six winters he had taught a district school,
   And had been quite successful in them all:
And nearly all the time his hands were full,
   Although 'twere possible he might recall
Some boyish scrapes that he was sometimes in,
Yet slowly upward had his progress been.

II.

And now we find him — well, he is a man,
   In growth of stature, though not fully grown
In intellect or morals yet, as can,
   In all such cases, be distinctly shown.
He hardly seems the boy we first began
   To talk about, whom now indeed we've known
A dozen years and more; nor is it he,
His former self, but what he's grown to be.

III.

So change is stamped upon us. Never mind!
   I still must follow him, and trust that you
May follow me. At first he had designed
   To enter college; but at length, in view

Of circumstances, which have oft combined,
  To crush our aspirations, old or new,
He gave it over, and began to read,
With earnest zeal, the Esculapian creed.

IV.

Which shows the structure of the human frame,
  From metatarsal bones to cerebellum;
To every bone and muscle gives its name,
  And teaches its disciples how to tell 'em;
To much superior wisdom makes its claim,
  And writes diplomas on its sheets of vellum,
The knowledge of the graduate to show,
Or make amends for what he doesn't know.

V.

Which teaches how to diagnose a case,
  Whene'er a case demands a diagnosis
To follow out the pathologic trace
  Of rheumatism, fever or necrosis;
And all diseases promptly to efface,
  Except incipient tuberculosis,
And such as lurk unseen and unsuspected,
Or prove defiant when they've been detected.

VI.

He entered as a student with a knight
  Of pill and powder, of reputed skill,
And used his leisure time as best he might,
  When he was teaching school or in the mill,
Until he was, in some respects, a quite
  Proficient scholar; or at least until
Prepared at length for gleaning further knowledge,
As student medical in Harvard College:

VII.

Which he'd designed to enter when he could,
  Or when he had the means that he could spare,
No other college seeming quite as good,
  His tutor having graduated there,
Though many years before. And now he stood
  So well financially that he could bear
The strain upon his purse, perhaps, and so
He felt that he was now prepared to go.

VIII.

He packed his clothes and books, and said good by,
  To Mrs. Reed, who long had been his friend,
Her little daughter who, with moistened eye,
  The parting kiss stood ready to extend,
The wise old doctor who had taught him why
  No human life should prematurely end,
If treated skilfully, *secundum artem* —
And other friends, as fortune now must part 'em.

IX.

He reached the city and procured a place
  For board and lodging, and matriculated —
As teachers call the entry to the race,
  Wherein aspiring youths are educated —
And paid the fees exacted in the case,
  A destiny to which we all are fated,
Except the privileged and favored class,
Who make the tour of life upon a pass.

X.

His boarding place was in a " private way,"
  Through which 'twas " dangerous" to pass, as said
Upon the corner house, which is to say,
  That while no real danger you may dread,

The corporation don't intend to pay
    The damage, if you get a broken head,
By some mishap with which you chance to meet,
Because the way is not a public street.

XI.

'Twas stipulated in the trade, that he
    Should have a room mate, who, he was assured,
Was just as nice as any one could be,
    And he was fortunate to have secured
One so agreeable; but he was free
    To say that any one would be endured,
As matter of necessity, and not
For such companionship as might be brought.

XII.

And so at once he moved into the room —
    The other fellow's room, all put to rights —
And as a bride awaits the absent groom,
    He waited for his chum; but love requites
The waiting of the bride, while here the gloom
    Could only be dispelled by fancy's flights,
And they were not sufficient to prevent
Some indications of his discontent.

XIII.

But 'twasn't long before the other came,
    And Mrs. Stearns came with him up the stairs;
The boarding mistress, a loquacious dame,
    And one well skilled in marketing her wares;
And she was praising Will about the same,
    Bestowing compliments in equal shares,
Perhaps deservedly, on either hand,
And coming in, she said, with smile so bland,

XIV.

"Now here's the dear old friend and here the new"—
    They stood in silence with a youthful grace —
"At least he's been here longer than have you"—
    Each looked a moment in the other's face —
"And now we like him as we do but few"—
    They raised their arms as if they would embrace;
And saying to himself, "It's him, it's him,"
One shouted, "Will," the other shouted, "Tim."

XV.

And sure enough, they knew each other, though
    So long a time since they had met before,
Despite the changes which impress us so,
    When boyhood fast approaches manhood's door;
The quite pretentious beard that Will could show
    Upon his face, which Tim declared was more
Becoming than his own, that wasn't quite
As well developed, but was rather light.

XVI.

"Now where the dickens have you been, Will, say?"
    Thus queried Tim when they were left alone;
"Why don't you write a fellow any way?
    How does it happen that I haven't known
That you were coming? Have you come to stay?
    What brought you here?" and in a lower tone,
"Did this soft soaper tell you I was here?
I like her pretty well, although she's queer."

XVII.

"No," Will replied, "she didn't tell me who
    Was here, but said a nice young fellow was;
How came you here? What did you come to do,
    Or have you done? I didn't write because

I didn't know that you were coming too;
   And thought I'd have my next contain a clause,
Reporting my arrival; so I waited,
To get here first, and get initiated."

XVIII.

"Initiated, say, what into, Will?"
   And Will explained to him the situation;
And Tim remarked that he had come to fill
   A vacant clerkship for an old relation;
An uncle living up on Beacon Hill,
   Who kept a grocery near where stands the station
The street cars start from now at Bowdoin Square,
And for the present he was working there.

XIX.

They told each other of the haps and chances,
   Which had befallen them since last they met;
And there are always some, as life advances,
   Of most absorbing interest, and yet,
To put them all on record, so enhances
   The scope of history, that I needs must let
Them all remain untold, or nearly all,
And only tell what further may befall.

XX.

The store had furnished Tim so much to do,
   'Twas difficult for him to get away;
For working through the day and evening too,
   Left little time to roam or read or play;
But he proposed before the week was through,
   To take a Sunday, if a pleasant day,
In spite of churches and of Christian rites,
To ramble over town and see the sights.

XXI.

And so they did; they wandered up and down,
  As 'twere at random, having no design
Of any kind, except to see the town,
  Which they regarded as exceeding fine:
And in a church that borrowed from the crown,
  Before the time of royalty's decline,
The name King's Chapel, in the afternoon,
They stopped to worship; and to there attune

XXII.

Their harps and hearts for singing Heaven's praise,
  To make some slight amends for violation
Of Heaven's law; and in accustomed ways,
  To thus discharge neglected obligation,
Considered due. They didn't even raise
  The question now so much in disputation,
Of human freedom, and the right to say,
By each, how each shall spend the Sabbath day.

XXIII.

And I have known religious devotees,
  Enthusiastic in their church devotions,
As inconsistent as were ever these
  Young fellows interviewing Boston notions;
Their hearts as thankful as the Pharisee's,
  That they are not like other men; emotions
Which I would not by any means condemn,
  For I am thankful not to be like them.

XXIV.

Next morning Will resumed his chosen task;
  And every day the busy season through,
He sought to penetrate beneath the mask
  That knowledge always wears. And what to do

Between the terms, he scarcely stopped to ask,
    But took the mill, the old position too,
To rest the intellect a while, and then
Came back to town and went to work again.

XXV.

He reached the middle of his final course
    Of study at the college, and he thought
That he'd discovered something of the source
    Of much disease which on the world was brought,
In other ways, as well as by the force
    Of injudicious eating; which is fraught
With danger now, as when, all fresh and nice
Good mother Eve ate fruit in paradise.

XXVI.

And she had one advantage over us,
    Her fruit had not been "deaconed" on the sly,
By some dishonest, enterprising c-ss,
    Who, in his dealings, lived a constant lie.
They hadn't got to doing business thus,
    They didn't ship their fruit to Boston, I
Conclude from what the record says about it,
And so the Hub must then have been without it.

XXVII.

And Willoughby had also read a few
    Historical and other books, beside
Materia Medica; and something knew
    Of past events, which charity should hide,
Except for sake of truth, which brings to view
    The ugly things that float upon the tide
Of human life, as well as those that shine,
On history's page, like diamonds in a mine.

XXVIII.

He could recite a poem or a speech,
    And do it pretty well, which made him some
Acquaintances more difficult to reach,
    By ordinary methods, in the hum
Of college life, where learned professors teach
    Their truths — and errors too — but go and come,
As teachers rather than associates,
Maintaining their superior estates.

XXIX.

He knew a young M. D. in Tremont Street,
    Who graduated several years before
Himself had entered; whom he chanced to meet,
    As he pursued his scientific lore,
A Dr. Hathaway, who had a suite
    Of rooms, consisting of a single floor,
Wherein he held receptions now and then,
Inviting in young women and young men,

XXX.

Of literary tastes, who had beside,
    Some taste for sociability, which they —
The Dr. and his wife — could well provide,
    For she was social — Mrs. Hathaway —
And could at parties gracefully preside,
    Though she was not particularly gay,
But suave and gentle, like the ladies we
Are most impressed with, whom we chance to see.

XXXI.

And Will had been invited once or twice,
    These social entertainments to attend;
And he regarded them as very nice,
    Although he much regretted that his friend

Was not invited too; but Tim's advice
   Was, "Go, Will, go, you see you cannot mend
The matter if you stay; and I don't care,
I'll be as happy somewhere else as there."

XXXII.

A happy faculty, which even I
   Have learned to cultivate, as year by year,
My friends grow less, and often pass me by,
   Since she who made their friendship seem sincere,
Beneath the moaning trees was doomed to lie,
   For with a love that "casteth out all fear,"
I look to that great source of love divine,
Whose light is shed on hearts like even mine.

XXXIII.

O thou, companion of my early days!
   My heart was first enamoured of the smile
That played upon thy lips: thine artless ways
   Seemed fraught with innocence and free from guile;
And thy maturer life deserves much praise,
   For virtues which adorned it all the while,
Until thy feet grew weary of the strife,
Which marks the progress here of human life.

XXXIV.

Above thy resting-place on yonder hill,
   No seeming presence breaks the loneliness; —
However thoughts of thee my bosom fill,
   That sacred soil my feet but seldom press;
I think of thee as living, smiling still;
   And seem to feel thy spirit's fond caress,
The benediction resting on my head,
Of one already risen from the dead.

XXXV.

We all have some resources not well known,
 To others or ourselves; that help us through
With many a sorrow under which we groan
 In spirit, for a time, and then renew
Life's struggles with a force not all our own,
 Which nature furnishes; perhaps in view
Of such necessity as comes to each,
For strength apparently beyond our reach.

XXXVI.

Will met one day with Dr. Hathaway,
 Who said to him, "Next Friday night again,
We have a sociable, and trust we may,
 Not vainly, count upon your presence then;
We shall expect to see you, and what say
 You as to giving us a specimen
Of your ability in recitation,
For entertainment or for information?"

XXXVII.

Will said he'd go, but rather be excused
 From taking any very active part,
As he was busy, and but little used
 To exercises in dramatic art;
They'd neither be enlightened nor amused
 By such small wares in literary mart,
As he could offer, though perhaps he'd try
And do a little something by and by.

XXXVIII.

But he was ready when the evening came,
 With such selection as he found at hand,
And so responded when they called his name,
 Though he was not the first to take the stand.

Another worthy youth, of local fame,
   A music teacher, gave upon demand,
Some past experiences — on deck and prow —
Of summer pleasures, though 'twas winter now.

THE GULNARE.

A SEASIDE IDYL.

Of all the pleasant things this world contains,
   And they in numbers are by no means few,
Of all the blessings which the Father rains
   On thankless mortals, such as I or you,
Of all the fond attractions here and there,
   Which interest us all in some degree,
Not least among the ones I fondly share,
   Are those which greet me by the mystic sea.

Invited by a friend one summer day,
   With him and other guests to take a sail,
Around the harbor, out upon the bay,
   I gladly answered that I would not fail.
And I was early at the rendezvous,
   The sky was bright as ever it could be,
The air was clear, the sun was shining through,
   And calmly resting on the peaceful sea.

There came upon the wharf a score or so,
   Of men and matrons, and of maidens fair,
Who in the tender took a quiet row,
   Which brought us safely to the yacht Gulnare.
And when the sails had all been duly set,
   When mainsail, jib and topsail all were free,
When they the mild and gentle breezes met,
   They bore us slowly out upon the sea.

And soon the flapping sails began to fill,
   The craft at length was fairly under way,
The winds increased, as did the waves, until
   The sails far over to the leeward lay;
And all were ordered by "the commodore,"
   To sit upon the windward side, as she,
The gallant barque, receding from the shore,
   Was being tossed upon the rolling sea.

We gazed upon each fast returning wave,
   And watched the greater ones, which never fail
To come in turn, whose breaking oft would lave
   The vessel's side, well up upon the rail;
And sometimes splashing over on the deck,
   With furious rage or in demoniac glee,
Seemed fond of threatening with instant wreck,
   Our tiny ship in the revengeful sea.

And yet in safety on the swelling tide,
   Although it made of us a seeming toy,
We traversed rapidly the waters wide,
   Beyond the beacon and the whistling buoy;
But, when far out upon the watery waste,
   Old father time recorded his decree,
That we must change our outward course, and haste
   From off the restless and the billowy sea.

There was a girl on board, with locks of gold,
   Who looked abroad from out a hazel eye,
Whose face seemed fashioned in so fair a mould,
   I scarce remember it without a sigh;
And when reclining on the forward deck,
   I thought at times she seemed to smile on me;
But then she gave the answering smile a check,
   And looked away into the surging sea.

O deep, dark sea! thy hungry waves contain
   Full many a foundered hope besides the one
Which, born and buried on the murmuring main,
   Thus briefly glistened in the noontide sun.
And many a moral barque which promised well,
   Is tossed about as we are tossed in thee;
And often wellnigh wrecked beneath the swell,
   And angry breakers of some moral sea.

Ah well! I did my best, and must suppress
   The vain regrets which sad remembrance brings;
All joys are tinged with sorrow more or less,
   And there must be an end to earthly things,
And so must end that long, bright, happy day;
   My harp must hang upon the willow tree,
But memory still may see from far away,
   The yacht Gulnare upon the swelling sea.

XXXIX.

When he was through, and one had cried, "Alas!"
  At his imaginary nonsuccess,
In bringing out what might have come to pass,
  And they had cheered the effort more or less.
A lady from a graduating class
  Of elocutionists, would now express
Some sentiments in blank verse written out,
Concerning which she seemed to have no doubt.

THE RACE OF LIFE.

This life is but a battle or a race,
In which the crowds rush furiously by,
And push and jostle on the king's highway;
Wherein we all do more or less contend
For triumph, or the prize we covet most.
  For pleasure oft, which doth the soul allure
To some sweet pastime or some promised joy.
But pleasures often end in bitter pain,
And those especially which violate
Some well known physical or moral law;
Or even laws unknown, until revealed
Through penalties incurred by violation.
  For wealth, that shall supply our pressing wants,
For food and raiment, shelter, house and home;
And that wherewith, in feebleness or age,
To keep the wolf of hunger from the door.
But from the exercise of frugal thrift,
Howe'er commendable, as in itself,
There may develop such a love of gain
As shall betray us to an evil doom.
So should we pray, as Agur did of old,
That neither poverty nor riches come
To us in great excess above our needs,
Lest peradventure with a gormand greed,
We seek for treasure for its own dear sake;
And in our miser chests do hoard it up,
And count the shining shekels o'er and o'er,
Until ourselves become almost a part
And parcel of the same; for wheresoe'er
The treasure is, the heart must also be,

Which thus is cankered by the greed of gold ;
If we indeed the golden prize should win.
    Ambition struggles for a doubtful fame,
And long endeavors to perpetuate
An unknown name unto the coming time,
By tongue or pen, or valiant deeds in war ;
Or even only monument of stone ;
Whereon has been engraven not alone
Hic jacet he whose ducats reared the shaft,
But all the good his character contained,
Is duly chronicled and noted down.
But monuments are not in good repute
For truthfulness; and even what they say,
Is oft unnoticed by the passers by.
Not only so, but time shall surely come,
When stony script shall not be legible;
Nay more, when granite shaft and marble slab,
Moss grown and old, shall crumble into dust.
When cruel deeds of war shall be unknown,
And be remembered only as the crimes
Which marred the records of a savage age.
    And is there nothing then of life, that lives
Beyond men's recollections of the past ?
Yea, yea, the consciousness of duty done;
The sure possession of a character
Unsullied by the stain of flagrant wrong.
Not only so, but one that bears the stamp
Of vigorous virtue and of righteousness.
A life unselfish, save as one may seek,
By reflex action from his noble deeds,
For self aggrandizement; for 'tis a law
Of nature's constitution, written down
In every human soul — if we have wit
Sufficient to enable us to read
In nature's statute books — that he who strives
For goodness in himself, and others' weal,
Shall find contentment, happiness and peace.
The race is won not always by the swift,
Nor is the battle to the strong alone;
But rather him who fights on virtue's side,
And him that in the right direction runs.
    The race for manhood and for womanhood,
Of noblest pattern and of highest type,
Although the obstacles to overcome,
Within ourselves and also from without,

Be great and numerous, is one whose lists
'Twere wise to enter in our early youth,
And run with patience till the goal is reached,
The object gained, the highest prizes won.
And when to him who runs in such a race,
The summons comes that comes to all, "to join
The innumerable caravan that moves
To the pale realms of shade," he goes to rest
" Like one who wraps the drapery of his couch
About him, and lies down to pleasant dreams."
And with the inner consciousness that he
Shall wake again beneath some fairer sky,
And only in restraint of virtue's bonds,
Which leave the virtuous untrammelled, walk
In peace and freedom on the hills of God.

XL.

Another lady still, whose lofty brow
  Was more expressive than we often see,
Who might have said, " I'm holier than thou,"
  But she was modest to a high degree —
A married dame — came slowly forward now,
  And gave some quite unusual thoughts, which she
Apparently believed in, as may you,
  Or not, as you may hold them false or true.

MARTIN LUTHER.

I stayed at a farm-house a couple of days,
  And they sent me to bed before ever 'twas dark;
And then in accord with their sensible ways,
  We all in the morning were up with the lark;

And casting about in my room for a glass,
  Wherein I could see in arranging my toilet,
If artful endeavor were bringing to pass
  The result I intended or tending to foil it,

Approaching the spot where I thought it should be,
  Between the two windows in front of the bed,
A picture of Luther looked down upon me,
  From a heavy gilt frame, and it served me instead.

For I saw that my face was reflected in his —
  Or the glass it was under — and coming still nearer,
In spite of his fame, as world-wide as it is,
  I used the old Wittenburg saint for a mirror.

Nor is it uncommon, I've come to believe,
  To see ourselves mirrored in other folks' faces,
Or characters either, so prone to deceive,
  In regard to their sins, or their virtues and graces.

We meet with a man of whom little we know,
  And ask him about his religion — or creed —
And he frankly avows his belief, so and so,
  And his tenets are such as most people concede

To be true, and if we, for the sake of applause,
  Or approval, pretend to believe the same thing,
While in fact, in our creed we've inserted a clause,
  That we haven't the courage to publicly fling

In the face of the world, we are apt to suspect
  That the other man too, is a moral pretender,
And in his professions we seem to detect
  A false faith, with another dishonest defender.

On the other hand, if, being true and sincere,
  We hear a consummate old hypocrite preach,
In the faith we have held for this many a year,
  Which he, for his living, is willing to teach,

We never suspect that with him it's a sham,
  That his heart of all dissimulation is full,
We hear but his prayer for the newly shorn lamb,
  While he is but warming himself in the wool.

A farmer comes in with potatoes and eggs,
  All carefully deaconed, the poorest to screen,
A calf that is cruelly tied by the legs,
  A horse that, like Cassius, looks hungry and lean,

And trading his produce and getting his pay,
  And whether or not they have happened to beat him,
He gets in his buggy, and driving away,
  Is likely to think that the village folks cheat him.

The village in turn, with its dissolute holes
   For drinking and gaming, declares it's a pity —
While fervently praying for other men's souls —
   That sin in all forms, is so rife in the city.

A book agent calls, it may be, at the door,
   And very politely exhibits his wares,
Containing all knowledge unwritten before,
   He seemingly very sincerely declares,

Persuading the honest and truthful good dame,
   As hungry for knowledge as grandmother Eve,
To give him her money, or give him her name,
   While he was presumably born to deceive.

Perchance a young maiden becomes an "old maid;" —
   And here I protest in humanity's name,
Against the low stigma thus sought to be laid
   On this worthy condition of unmarried dame,

By such gross appellation. I honor the woman
   Who, forty years old, on a platform, or stage,
Although, as she said, 'twas a little uncommon,
   Announced to the public that she was of age.

That she should assume the grown title of Mrs.,
   And shouldn't respond any longer to Miss;
And why should a world so enlightened as this is,
   Not recognize such a position as this?

And then to defend it, and give us her views in
   Regard to the matter, at length she went on,
"If Susan B. Anthony still is Miss Susan,
   Why don't they call Whittier still Master John?"

She deemed it an outrage, and treated it so,
   That a matron is Missed like a girl in her youth,
Thus answering whether she's married or no,
   As if it were somebody's business, in sooth.

When a boy is of age, or before, it may be,
   It is deemed but polite to address him as Mr.;
And that is all right as all seem to agree,
   And all practise it too; but his unmarried sister,

Through barbarous custom, must ever ignore
    The fact of her womanhood, simply because
That for better or worse, she's not taken some more
    Or less promising youth; and the infamous laws

Of society make it appear a disgrace —
    Though 'tis oft the reverse — and the fact must be hurled,
On every occasion, direct in her face,
    And direct in the face of a curious world.

But excuse this digression. I say if a maiden
    Sips not at the cup of young marital bliss,
She still must regard it, we think, as her aiden,
    Which she, by misfortune, has happened to miss.

For the average woman and average man,
    Thus seeing themeslves, as reflected in others,
See no other reason why nature's old plan,
    That was wisely pursued by their fathers and mothers,

Should not have been also pursued in the case
    Under consideration, excepting the one,
Peradventure, that she was outrun in the race,
    Or had been, by some prosperous rival, outdone.

A lady residing in Claremont, has,
    As she says, quite a habit of studying faces;
Expressing her views in regard to them, as
    She is pleased or displeased with the ones that she traces.

And riding one day in a car, she observed
    That a lady, though sitting some distance away,
Was glancing at her; and her countenance served
    For a short commentary, wherein she might say

Whatsoever she pleased. "What a great homely face!
    So broad, so expressionless, stupid," she said,
" And she's looking at me with a rather bad grace; "
    And she noticed, on raising her hand to her head,

That the other one too, did exactly the same:
    "Oh dear!" she exclaimed, with an audible groan,
" Do I know my own face ? do I know my own name ? "
    For she looked in a mirror: the face was her own.

There's much in the world we are prone to condemn,
   We grumble at people and things as they pass,
But while we are laughing and sneering at them,
   We oftentimes see but ourselves in a glass.

XLI.

An oldish man, who owned the house wherein
   The doctor's suite of rooms was situate,
Who oft had kindly and politely been,
   As now, invited to participate,
Who had a strong dislike for whiskey, gin
   And so forth, now proceeded to relate,
Or rather from his manuscript he read,
This temperance story, which was true, he said.

A WESTERN GIRL.

My heroine's a girl, unknown to fame,
   Unknown to me since many years ago,
Except that recently I've heard her name,
   In such connection as may serve to show
That she had character and sterling worth,
When only twenty summers from her birth.

Her father earned his living, during youth
   And early manhood, making boots and shoes;
Her mother too, to ne'er disguise the truth,
   Entangled fast in matrimony's noose,
With little store of worldly wealth, 'twas said,
Made hats and bonnets for her daily bread.

An honest calling — honestly pursued —
   Was his or hers, whereby, between the two,
They kept the wolf at bay, and oft renewed
   The empty larder with a hat or shoe,
For which we all have more or less a passion,
To suit the season or the coming fashion.

They prospered fairly well from year to year,
   And she was satisfied, or seemed to be;
But he was longing for a new career —
   From present occupations to be free;
He sought, in short, from stubborn fate to wrench
A higher station than the Crispin's bench.

He figured up his then outstanding claims,
  He sold his kit, which wasn't quite his all,
In bold pursuance of his lofty aims,
  A move quite difficult to now recall —
A metamorphosis already past,
By which the shoe he'd made, became his last.

He cast about for something else to do,
  Although the search was bootless for a time,
But, various enterprises conning through,
  He said at length, with purposes sublime,
The clerical profession he'd embrace,
And preach the gospel to a sinful race.

The change was but a slight one after all,
  For even now 'twas but repairing souls,
That had been injured by a dangerous fall,
  Of chronic standing — mending moral holes
In moral garments, often worn so thin,
'Twere hard to tell where he had best begin.

But just before his ordination day,
  Foreordination seemed to intervene,
And put the former, for the time, away,
  So far away, in fact, 'twas never seen;
For, hoping thus to reap more golden fruits,
He then engaged in mercantile pursuits.

And afterwards in speculating schemes;
  In heavy contracts, and in western lands;
Wherein he prospered even beyond the dreams
  Of wealth, with which his fancy filled his hands;
Until he settled, as he deemed it best,
In some new city of the growing west.

Meanwhile the wife, our heroine's good mother,
  Had steadily pursued her old vocation;
The child and she, who dearly loved each other,
  Sustaining still the natural relation
Which nature gave them, in their quiet home,
With no desire in distant lands to roam.

But now, the father having settled down,
  A wealthy citizen, or well-to-do
At least, in such a busy, far-off town
  As he was in, the wife and daughter too,

Must needs go thither, as anon they did;
As wives are wont to go where husbands bid.

And so the millinery goods were sold,
  As also was the shop, which she had earned
By substituting new things for the old;
  And now their steps were gladly, sadly turned
In the direction of the setting sun,
Where new lives, as it were, should be begun.

A new, commodious house, which had been reared
  For their reception, on a pleasant bluff,
That overlooked the river, wild and weird,
  Containing household goods in *quamtum suff*—
With open doors stood ready to enfold,
And shelter them from rain and wind and cold.

And here they lived; and she, the growing maiden,
  Whose culture had by no means been neglected,
Performed the tasks with which her hands were laden,
  No less acceptably than was expected,
Sustaining all her various parts so well,
She soon became a noted city belle.

In social gatherings the echoes rang,
  Of many a genial air she'd played and sung,
For well she played, melodiously sang,
  And fluently conversed, for one so young,
But more especially did she advance,
In graceful movements in the mazy dance.

And so it chanced, in a commodious hall,
  The yearly "Christmas hop" had been announced,
And all the belles were there, or nearly all,
  In costly dresses, duly fringed and flounced,
A brilliant gathering of the city's best
And Clara prominent among the rest.

And some aspiring devotee had brought
  His genius into play, and had invented
A daring scheme, in wildest fancy wrought,
  By which some novel scenes should be presented;
And had erected there, his power to own,
The fabled wine god, on a gilded throne.

And these were in a sylvan bower, reared
  To serve his purpose, fronting down the hall,

And when each couple in the waltz, appeared
   Before its door, the sceptered hand would fall,
And beck them in, to worship at his shrine,
   And proffer her a goblet filled with wine.

And she in turn, receiving it from him,
   Was then expected in her place to stand,
And sipping daintily the goblet's brim,
   To give it then into her partner's hand;
And thereupon, in bacchanalian trance,
He quaffed the nectar and resumed the dance.

Now Clara had received as living truth,
   The temperance teachings of her native home;
And when she looked upon the generous youth
   Who waltzed with her, and then upon the dome
Of Bacchus' bower, as they approached the spot,
She trembled slightly, though she faltered not.

Her face was for a moment overcast
   With doubtful shadows, which anon grew less,
For almost instantly the doubts were past,
   The purpose fixed which she would soon express;
And she resumed her wonted ease and grace,
And calmly stood in her allotted place:

Where those preceding her had stood, within
   The charmed enclosure, thus in beauty wrought,
But being dedicated now to sin,
   With much of danger and of sorrow fraught,
Though wooed so thoughtlessly by gallant swain,
Who sowed for pleasure, but may reap with pain.

She took the goblet, not from willing choice,
   But from a conscious duty would not shrink,
And then repeating in a clear, strong voice,
   "Woe unto him that gives his neighbor drink,"
Behind the mimic throne she stood before,
She threw the wine cup down upon the floor.

And her New England mother, when she learned,
   The following morning, what the girl had done,
Did not withhold the praise which she had earned,
   "Of all your deeds it is the noblest one."
She fondly said, "and I am proud to know
You gave the scheme its partial overthrow."

All honor then, in this our sinful earth,
  To noble minded women who shall dare,
By word or action — even in scenes of mirth —
  To preach the temperance gospel everywhere.
If fall we must, O let us not repeat,
The woman gave it me and I did eat.

God speed the day when we may surely know
  That entertainment shall forego its wine;
And when the cup, with all its wealth of woe,
  Shall not be pressed to your lips or to mine;
And may the angels join the chorus then,
And sing of peace on earth, good will to men.

XLII.

His story listened to with much respect,
  And close attention, by his hearers, they,
Not pausing on its lesson to reflect,
  Now gladly turned to Mrs. Hathaway,
Who seldom read, but when she did select,
  Had always something she desired to say,
And now her theme, of childhood, youth and age,
Was one of interest to child or sage.

GRANDMA AND ADA.

GRANDMA was old and Ada was young;
  O'er Grandma's life, with its hopes and fears,
The mists of time long shadows had flung,
  She had lived for seven-and-sixty years,

When Ada was born; and in ten years more,
  Was a long way past threescore and ten,
Which sages recorded in days of yore,
  As the time allotted to women and men.

And Ada then was a laughing child:
  Her heart was swelling with mirth and glee,
Her ways, sometimes, were wayward and wild,
  But she lovingly sat on Grandma's knee,

And her warm, soft hand, with a childish grace,
    She often playfully pushed about,
Across the faded and wrinkled face,
    And tried to "iron the wrinkles out."

"Do you remember, Gran'ma," said she,
    "When you was a little girl of ten?
Did you have a smooth, round face, like me?
    Did you have a gran'ma, Gran'ma, then?

"Shall I be wrinkled as you are now?
    Shall I grow old, as you say all do?
I suppose I shall, but I don't see how;
    Shall I be a gran'ma, Gran'ma, too?"

"Nobody can tell about that, my dear;
    Go bring my staff from the corner there,"
She said, and her smile concealed a tear,
    As she slowly rose from the old arm chair,

And the two together went, hand-in-hand,
    Out into the yard, in the bright sunlight,
And looked at the sky, so blue and grand
    To the childish eye, while the inner sight

Of age looked through. 'Twas a glad sunrise
    And a calm sunset, in the mystic whirl
Of progressive life: one old and wise,
    The other was then but a fair-haired girl.

But when she arrived at "sweet sixteen,"
    Her old companion had passed away,
To the "Summer-land," and the turf was green,
    'Neath which the body of Grandma lay.

And oft in the golden sunset glow,
    By the marble stone on the churchyard hill,
A girlish form was bending low,
    And a loving heart was beating still.

And a prayer went up from quivering lips,
    To the Father's throne in the spirit land,
As a fresh bouquet of wild flower slips
    Dropped lovingly from Ada's hand.

O ceaseless time! on swiftest wing,
  Thou fliest past, as the records show;
Summer and winter, fall and spring,
  In quick succession come and go.

O tide of life! whereon we float,
  Until, as the silent warder calls,
We come at length to the shadowy moat,
  Surrounding the future's gilded walls.

Now Ada sits by the ingleside,
  And knits and sings. Her slippered toe
Moves up and down in the bright noontide,
  And a cradle is rocking to and fro.

A child, a maid, a bride, a — well,
  'Tis a mystic veil we cannot see through;
What the future holds, no one can tell,
  But Ada may "be a grandma too."

XLIII.

This, too, was cheered, with not a little zest,
  Which Will regarded rather unpropitious,
For he was called upon, and fearing, lest
  His own selection had been injudicious,
He rose and took his place, and did his best,
  And to excel was more or less ambitious,
As he related what we well may deem
The vague imaginations of a dream.

A DREAM.

I dreamed a queer dream, and a small, yellow cur,
  Came out with a growl, from between the two houses
Just over the way, and before I could stir,
  He had planted his teeth in the leg of my trousers.

And when I laid hold of the nape of his neck,
  And on the stone pavement ferociously threw him,
A savage old mastiff leaped off from the deck
  Of a steamer hard by, and proceeded to chew him

So mercilessly that I hadn't the heart
  To see the poor cur, that myself had just beaten,
So unfairly used, and I took the dog's part,
  As he, but for that, would no doubt have been eaten.

And so the world goes, that whoever is down,
  Gets most of the kicks, and the most of the bruises,
While he that can scarcely keep off from the town,
  Must pay for the goods that his rich neighbor uses.

I dreamed a wild dream, and the sky was o'ercast
  With the blackest of clouds, and they hung on the border,
With sullen forebodings, or hurrying past,
  Were chasing each other in wildest disorder.

At length the swift wind like a hurricane blew,
  And a lofty church steeple, all garnished and gilded,
Came down; and methought the old parable true,
  Of the house in the sand, which the foolish man builded.

Not only the wind, but the lightning's red glare,
  And the rain in huge torrents so swiftly descended,
And peals of loud thunder oft rended the air,
  Till the earth and the sky in wild chaos were blended.

When the storm had come on I was out for a ride,
  With a dappled bay span and an old-fashioned carriage;—
A charming young heiress sat close by my side,
  And the very next day was that fixed for our marriage.

The horses were borrowed, the carriage was mine,
  A sort of heir-loom an old uncle had given,
When he, for some reason, was in a decline,
  In fact, just before his departure for heaven.

And so as a family relic, 'twas prized,
  Though more, perhaps, out of respect to the giver;
But crossing a bridge the whole structure capsized,
  And I barely escaped a wet grave in the river.

The carriage went down, but the crash and the roar,
  Had frightened the steeds to a furious canter,
And so with a spring, they got safely on shore,
  As did the gray mare that bore off Tam O'Shanter.

The maiden was drowned, and I stood in despair,
  And gazed at her picture encased in a locket;
Though she was an heiress, I wasn't her heir,
  And her money was yet in her grandfather's pocket.

I dreamed a droll dream, and a pig from the sty
    Had escaped in affright, at the sight of a drover;
And coming along to a cask of "old rye,"
    At a grocer's back door, he just rooted it over.

Then a temperance lecture this four-footed Gough
    Commenced with a word which I cannot quite utter,
Meanwhile the main hoops of the barrel came off,
    And the poisonous fluid ran down in the gutter.

Now piggie, beware of the merciless laws
    Of the rumseller's code, to which you are a stranger,
And when you enlist in the temperance cause,
    Remember therein is a good deal of danger.

The grocer ran out with a murderous knife,
And straight to poor piggie's brave heart would have sent it,
And he as a martyr had laid down his life,
But I waked from my dream just in time to prevent it.

XLIV.

Will took his seat amid some kindly cheers,
    Expressive of a fair appreciation,
Though he himself still entertained some fears
    That he had not deserved much commendation;
Then came a lady, bowed with seeming years,
    And she was heralded by proclamation,
That she would sing of happy childhood's days,
And of the mystery of nature's ways.

XLV.

A young man played, as an accompanist,
    A small harmonica; and seemed to know
That 'twas his duty only to assist,
    And not to see how loudly he could blow,
As often does the modern melodist,
    In such a part, but rather, soft and low,
The notes which seconded the plaintive strain,
Wherein she sang the following refrain:

WILLOUGHBY'S WISDOM.

While sitting here in the gloaming,
  My heart is far away,
In the far off time 'tis roaming,
  When I was a child at play.
But time and tide wait never,
  For child or man, they say,
And flying, flowing ever,
  They find me old and gray.

O days of happy childhood,
  When hearts and hands were free,
When meadow, hill and wildwood
  Had many a charm for me!
The light of thy sun has vanished,
  The light of the morning star,
And men and women are banished,
  From childhood's world afar.

While sitting here in the gloaming,
  My heart is far away,
In olden memories roaming,
  When youth and love held sway;
But time doth never tarry,
  For age or youth I know,
The joys our young lives carry,
  They all must quickly go.

O days when vows are plighted,
  When love's young tendrils twine,
When heart to heart is united,
  By what they have deemed divine!
But the heart of its love grows weary,
  And love in its turn grows cold,
Or the autumn of life comes dreary,
  And lovers, alas! grow old.

While sitting here in the gloaming,
  My heart is far away,
In by-gone days 'tis roaming,
  The days that would not stay;
For time doth never linger,
  He flieth even now,
And writes with iron finger,
  Sad tales on cheek and brow.

And still I am dreaming, dreaming,
　Of the halcyon days of yore,
Of the joys behind me gleaming,
　And those which are still before;
The golden days of the future,
　The soul world whither we go,
The web of life without suture
　Of sorrow or pain or woe.

XLVI.

While thus she sang, with voice unbroken, sweet
　And clear, Will wondered if he couldn't trace
Some false appearances, though quite complete;
　She bore the years with well becoming grace,
And yet he queried if 'twere aged feet,
　That bore away the seeming wrinkled face;
Or if some girl had deemed it free from blame,
To play the role of venerable dame.

XLVII.

She disappeared, and after one or two
　More recitations, which had been requested,
Were creditably rendered, and were through,
　And satisfaction duly manifested,
Debating what 'twere further best to do,
　An enterprising genius then suggested,
If there was nothing more to say or sing,
They play a game of "thimble-in-the-ring."

XLVIII.

A game of forfeits; and the forfeiture,
　Therein exacted, I may safely say,
Although 'twas called a "judgment," to be sure,
　Was so prescribed, and paid in such a way,

As rendered it the charm which should allure
    A youthful company into the play:
And this was partly youthful, partly more
Advanced in years, as we have seen before.

XLIX.

But this did not defeat the proposition,
    Which was accepted with some slight demur;
And one or two, who favored prohibition
    Of such undignified amusements, were
Induced to take a hand, upon condition
    That judgments shouldn't rest on him or her,
Or them, if those in search should be so nimble
As, in their hands, to find the flying thimble:

L.

Which, when the play began, went round and round,
    A while so slyly as to give no sign,
To indicate its presence; but 'twas found,
    At length, by accident and by design,
With Dr. Hathaway; and he was bound,
    To suffer judgment or to pay his fine,
And so was sentenced to St. Peter's dome,
That is, to choose a mate and "go to Rome."

LI.

He chose as partner, the retiring maid,
    From the arena, who had found the prize
In his possession; who should thus be paid,
    As he remarked, for being so unwise.
Were that the heaviest burden ever laid
    On human shoulders, we could exercise
More patience and more willingness to bear
What might be reckoned as an equal share.

LII.

She seemed a pretty girl of twenty-two,
  Or may be twenty-three or twenty-four;
And when she came before my hero, who
  Had been presented to her by the door,
On coming in, he rose, that he might do
  His part politely, though he saw no more
About her then, of beauty's fair impress,
Than many another lady might possess.

LIII.

Her face he wasn't interested in,
  At first appearance, more especially
Than he might easily enough have been
  In those of other girls he chanced to see.
It was remarked to him she came from Lynn,
  Which has some pleasant memories for me,
Though having none for him — at least not then —
Through which to call past pleasures up again.

LIV.

And yet she had a certain native grace,
  That's better calculated to command
Appreciation than a pretty face;
  And when he touched her shoulder with his hand,
He felt a presence which he couldn't trace,
  Upon her countenance, or understand;
But he imagined, though he might be wrong,
That possibly 'twas she that sang the song.

LV.

And when she tendered him the modest kiss,
  That each received in turn, he felt a thrill
Of pleasure which, though not exactly bliss,
  Was quite sufficient for the time, to fill

His cup of earthly happiness; and this,
  Though frequently the harbinger of ill,
He half regarded as an indication
Of mutual love; at least in expectation.

LVI.

O thrill of love! thou art a fickle guest;
  Thy visits are but few and transitory;
Thou comest not at any known behest,
  And comest not to stay, except in story:
Thou hast been felt in almost every breast,
  Yet thine is but a momentary glory,
Which then subsides and quickly fades away,
Like sunset grandeur of a summer's day.

LVII.

As an emotion, love is but a myth,
  Or little better than a myth, at most;
Although at first it rears its monolith,
  And of the temple seems the corner post;
And binds the heart as by a birchen wyth,
  But vanishes as quickly as a ghost;
And breaks as easily as wyths around
The giant Samson, whom Delillah bound.

LVIII.

But as a principle it may be true,
  And more continuous; but Will, as yet,
Was not in love, so far as then he knew,
  Although he was entangled in the net
(Whose meshes thus entangle not a few),
  Which had been unintentionally set —
At least it didn't seem to be intended,
Though fate's design may not be apprehended.

LIX.

While in the game he subsequently sought
    For opportunity to do again,
That which, on this occasion, had been fraught
    With fascinating pleasure. Now and then
She came into his presence, and he thought
    She seemed to kindly smile upon him when
Good taste would sanction it, whenever they
Were brought together in the merry play.

LX.

But neither with his planning nor desire,
    To somehow bring about another kiss,
Would changing circumstances so conspire,
    As to accomplish it. He seemed to miss
The half recurring chances, though the fire,
    Enkindled by the other, was, I wis,
Still burning in his bosom, all aglow,
And seeking fuel which should keep it so.

LXI.

And so it happened, when the play was done,
    That ere he left, he got her private ear,
In conversation, and had soon begun
    To cultivate her friendship in sincere
And honest fashion; though as any one,
    Not yet at least designing to appear
More friendly than legitimately might
A stranger, well bred, civil and polite.

LXII.

He'd then forgotten what they called her name,
    As he remarked on sitting down beside her;
He'd heard them call her Nellie in the game,
    And she informed him it was Nellie Ryder.

He said he hoped it might remain the same,
   Until the best of fortune should betide her,
In changing it for one of equal merit,
With all the joy such changes e'er inherit.

LXIII.

He hoped that furthermore, ere that should be,
   Their slight acquaintance might be more complete;
And she responded she was glad to see
   Those whom she knew, and whom she chanced to meet;
But now 'twas evidently fate's decree,
   That they must part; so, rising from his seat,
He bowed politely, not to be remiss,
And said good night without a second kiss.

LXIV.

Some two weeks later, when the mail came round,
   The pennypost delivery of the day,
Among his letters — two or three — he found
   A hasty note from Dr. Hathaway.
The words were few, but had a thrilling sound,
   For very briefly he went on to say,
"As soon as 'tis convenient, please come in
And see me; we're invited down to Lynn."

LXV.

He didn't look around for hack or "bus,"
   And street cars then were scarcely yet invented.
They didn't carry as they carry us,
   For revenues so rapidly augmented,
By men whose measures we may not discuss,
   Whose capital is heavily per cented,
In Metropolitan and Highland shares,
Which long oppressed the poor with extra fares.

LXVI.

O greed of gold! thou knowest nor high nor low,
    Except the height and depth of coffers filled
With shining treasure till they overflow,
    And their possessors' equipages gild,
With all the regal splendor princes know,
    And many a huge palatial mansion build
In countries which all kingly power disown,
Though human rights be largely overthrown.

LXVII.

When Garfield fell, by murder's cruel deed,
    Men gathered round to save a fallen brother,
The world devoutly prayed they might succeed,
    As well the stranger as the aged mother.
The doctors came to help him in his need,
    The ball went one way, they probed in the other,
And the exact position it was in,
They promptly told us in their bulletin.

LXVIII.

And when at last death claimed him for its own,
    As eagles gather "where the carcass is,"
Each vampire had a mighty vulture grown,
    To prey upon all human maladies,
And with a greed that had been seldom shown,
    Now deemed that half the country's wealth was his,
Because he sought to cure or helped to kill,
The wounded President whose pulse was still.

LXIX.

The nation yet, the other patient dead,
    Is being treated for her chronic bane,
The treatment such as doctors long were bred
    To, namely, that of opening a vein;

And she alas! so often has been bled,
   She seems to feel no loss, or sense of pain,
But yields herself a nonresisting prey,
   While slowly ebbs her waning life away.

LXX.

'Twas in the morning Will received the word,
   Some time before the lectures would begin;
And he was curious, from what he'd heard,
   To know who 'twas inviting them to Lynn,
Although in guessing he could not have erred,
   As there was no one else it could have been,
And yet he started at a rapid pace,
To ask the Dr. more about the case.

LXXI.

Miss Ryder was a relative of his,
   The doctor's — or related to his wife,
As nearly as a second cousin is,
   And she besides, had known her all her life;
And now a meeting of the families
   Had been proposed to keep old memories rife;
And Nellie to the doctor had suggested
That Will, in whom he seemed quite interested,

LXXII.

Might be invited if he thought he would
   Regard it as a privilege to come,
Though there was no great reason why he should,
   As the attractions, at the *maximum*,
Would be but little that a stranger could
   Enjoy, unless he magnified them some,
Which she, perhaps, had felt she might expect him
To do, unless the doctor should neglect him.

LXXIII.

The doctor said, "Although a little shy,
   I think she's interested in you, too,
And you, I venture now to prophesy,
   Will be the only one invited who
Is not related. She assumed 'twas I
   That wanted you to go, and so I do,
As I've requested you, but she, I guess,
Is also looking for you none the less."

LXXIV.

Will said he should be glad to think 'twas so,
   And in his inner consciousness was glad
Of what there was of evidence to show
   That 'twas, or of the little proof he had;
And he at once decided he would go,
   And trust to fortune and to chance to add
Somewhat of interest to that which he
Believed was mutual in some degree.

LXXV.

And when the day the invitation named,
   At length arrived, he found himself in Lynn;
A handsome city, which has long been famed
   For handsome shoes the world is standing in;
Although perhaps so much should not be claimed,
   For beauty of its women. There have been,
However, some within that goodly city,
Whom I have known, and have esteemed them pretty.

LXXVI.

He strolled about, with nothing else to do,
   And in the window of a large shoe store,
He saw a badly worn and cast off shoe,
   The upper half divided from the lower,

By being ripped till nearly torn in two,
   The two parts standing like an open door,
Or partly open one, somewhat distended,
Until it might be deemed past being mended.

LXXVII.

The pegs were standing in a double row,
   Their number having seemingly increased,
So many being in the sole below,
   The upper having none the less, at least,
Like rows of teeth that dogs are wont to show,
   The whole resembling some ferocious beast,
Or reptile, such as come from the equator;
And this was labelled a "Lynn alley gaiter."

LXXVIII.

Will stood a minute to admire the pun,
   And laugh at such a comical invention,
At least it seemed to him so cute a one
   As to be worth an incidental mention;
And when he turned in the declining sun,
   A customer attracted his attention;
For he discovered Nellie Ryder there,
Among the boots, and trying on a pair.

LXXIX.

When he went in, she proffered him her hand —
   "I'm not quite ready yet for company,
But shall be soon," she said, with manner bland,
   And added, "then I'll take you home with me."
And he was at her service on demand —
   "But let me get my other boot," said she,
"I have but one, and I shall need the other,
Though first I'll introduce you to my mother."

LXXX.

A woman nearly fifty years of age,
   Whom Will had scarcely noticed sitting there,
Or scarcely seen, now came upon the stage,
   And though some gray was sprinkled in her hair,
She still was handsome; and she could engage
   In conversation with a genial air,
But Will was disappointed thus to find
Her there, for he was conning in his mind,

LXXXI.

Some sentimental sentences to use,
   When he and Nellie should be on the way
To Nellie's home; and fate would now refuse
   The opportunity, and say him nay:
And as the mother they could not excuse,
   The interesting things that he would say,
Must all, for now at least, remain unsaid,
Although they still kept running in his head.

LXXXII.

At length they stood before the residence
   Of Julius Ryder on a quiet street,
A plain two story house, a picket fence,
   Enclosing grounds commodious and neat,
An elm tree standing by the gate, and thence
   A gravel walk, wherein they chanced to meet
With Mr. Ryder, near the portico,
When Nellie said, " My father you must know,

LXXXIII.

'Tis Mr. Hayden, he's the doctor s friend;
   The doctor's folks are coming by and by;
He left him making calls at the South End,
   But said they'd come to tea, at least would try,

Which, if you will excuse me, I will lend
  A hand in getting ; but so please you, I
Will take your coat first," she remarked to Will,
As they were entering the domicile.

LXXXIV.

So he took off his coat and followed her
  Along the hall to where the hat-tree was,
And when they were alone, he said, " You were
  Most kind to summon me, no doubt because
The Dr. knew me, and I should demur,
  Perhaps, against so indirect a clause
In the indictment." She replied, " O no,
You're quite mistaken, for it wasn't so.

LXXXV.

" I asked you simply that I wanted you
  To come; and here in our suburban home,
Our slight acquaintance to perhaps renew,
  To some extent, but now I'll let you roam
A little by yourself; " and he, in view
  Of love's fair fane, of turret, tower and dome,
As he imagined, strolled through room and hall,
Until the bell announced another call.

LXXXVI.

As they expected, ere 'twas time for tea,
  At least before the table had been laid,
The Dr. came, as well as two or three
  More city friends, by public coach conveyed,
And after supper, when both land and sea
  Were being mantled by the deepening shade,
Some others living nearer by, came in,
Who were at once their neighbors and their kin.

LXXXVII.

And when their hats and things were laid aside,
    And they were seated in a winding row,
They chatted cheerily of wind and tide,
    Of haps and happenings, as matters go,
How things were moving in the world so wide,
    Of their affairs, which can't be mine, you know,
Except to say the visit speeded well,
Including several games of bagatelle.

LXXXVIII.

The board was large and quite elaborate,
    And stood upon a large piano in
The small back parlor, and it had of late,
    Been brought by Nellie's uncle back to Lynn,
From his sojournings by the Golden Gate
    Of California, where he had been,
And whither he had gone. And he had said
It might be hers whenever she should wed.

LXXXIX.

Will played with Nellie and the Dr.'s wife,
    Against the Dr. and two other men,
Though in his own experience in life,
    He'd never witnessed such a game till then,
And yet so nearly equal was the strife,
    That, though they lost the "rubber game," 'twas when,
As seeming triumph was about to greet them,
The Dr. made a lucky score and beat them.

XC.

Will often wished that he could get a chance
    To interview Miss Nellie when alone,
Thereby his future prospects to enhance,
    And she had aspirations of her own;

But they had made no very marked advance,
 Unless, indeed, the seeds were being sown,
Which might, perhaps, develop by and by,
Although too early yet to prophesy.

XCI.

He did, however, playing bagatelle,
 Or rather when the triple game was ended,
Conduct his private enterprise so well,
 That he accomplished what he had intended,
To some extent, for when the last ball fell
 Upon its resting place, and was suspended,
And they had voted to suspend the play,
He turned to Nellie and went on to say,

XCII.

"It's quite a pretty game, though new to me,
 And quite a pretty place, your little city;
At least that part of it which I could see,
 In my brief wanderings." "And 'tis a pity,"
She said, "they were so brief. If I may be
 A self appointed, self controlled committee
Of invitation, I'll invite you, when
You can conveniently, to come again.

XCIII.

"You'd like to clamber up upon the brow
 Of old High Rock, or stroll along the shore;"—
He turned his eyes and saw that they were now
 More by themselves than they had been before,
And in an undertone he said, "Somehow
 I feel the more inclined to come, the more
I am persuaded; and if you will go
And see these places with me, which, you know,

XCIV.

"To interesting objects lends a charm,
    I'd like to come and see them by and by,
When spring advances till the sun is warm
    Until the ground is also warm and dry,
When strolling out of doors will do no harm,
    And be enjoyable." In her reply,
She frankly said, as soon as he was through,
"I'm sure I should be very happy to."

XCV.

No sooner were the words, however, spoken,
    Than some one came into the atmosphere
Surrounding them; and so the spell was broken,
    Though Nellie's eye was moistened with a tear;
Which might have been regarded as a token
    Of more than was permitted to appear
Upon the surface; as the heart may feel,
At times, what prudence prompts us to conceal.

XCVI.

Nor did the evening furnish opportunity
    For further conversation, saving such
As was appropriate to their community
    Of social interests. However much
There might have been of that celestial unity
    Of feeling which surroundings cannot touch,
They couldn't give expression to it, so
If it were felt or not, they didn't know.

XCVII.

And when twas time that they must say good by,
    They knew not whether each had found a friend.
They looked inquiringly, but no reply
    From either came, which they could comprehend;

And there was no embrace, no kiss, no sigh,
   Naught save what true politeness might intend
As mere civility; and still in doubt,
They shook hands, said good night, and he went out.

XCVIII.

When he was gone, and she had shut the door,
   Her father said, "My dear, is that some beau
You've lately found, or one you've known before?"
   She said, "I should be satisfied to know
That he was either one. He'll come once more,
   I think, and then I'll try to make him so,
Against which he, however, may protest;"
Which might have been in earnest or in jest.

XCIX.

Will reached the city by the Eastern train,
   Which then arrived a little after ten,
And queried if his trip had been in vain,
   Or if 'twere worth his while to go again —
A mental question, coming from the brain,
   The heart as promptly answering that when
Occasion favored it, he'd try and win
Some further conquests on the shores of Lynn.

C.

When at his boarding place, his smiling chum,
   Who wasn't yet in bed, accosted him,
"Hello, my friend, I'm very glad you've come,
   Is love's star growing bright, or growing dim?"
Will ordinarily was pretty mum,
   In such affairs, but wasn't so with Tim;
And frankly answered him, "It glimmers yet,
It hasn't risen much, nor has it set."

CI.

He then detailed to him the circumstances
   Connected with the visit just concluded,
To show that it contained not many chances
   To ascertain if he had been deluded,
As he could make but very few advances —
   "And she, I dare say, made no more than you did,"
Suggested Tim; "why not sit down and write her?
   Or you might make a party and invite her; —

CII.

"A literary party, such as these
   You're having now at Dr. Hathaway's,
Where you would be at home and quite at ease,
   As well in letters as the coming plays.
I'll give a recitation if you please,
   Of some old warrior's deeds or poet's lays,
Some great oration or some little verse,
Which, if we had a rostrum, I'd rehearse."

CIII.

He went and took a drawer from the sink,
   And turned it bottom upwards on the floor,
And standing on it, seemed to try to think
   Of some old declamation, learned of yore,
That might supply a necessary link,
   In such proceedings. Then he said, "Encore!
I'll give 'em that 'Old Fifer,' that will do;"
And he commenced, and thus rehearsed it through.

THE OLD FIFER.

No longer we hear the old fifer play
   The martial music he loved so much,
The shrill notes which, for many a day,
   Had answered oft to the magic touch

Of his wrinkled fingers, long and lean,
    Yet losing none of their old-time skill,
In conjuring up from realms unseen,
    The fairy forms of the master's will.

Although his fingers were lean and long,
    The finger of time had made them so,
For they were supple and full and strong,
    In the halcyon days of long ago;
For now it is three score years and ten —
    The time allotted to human life —
Since Uncle Perry — a stripling then —
    Began to play the inspiring fife.

When John Bull came to our north frontier,
    Unfurling his flag in the noontide gleam,
When the roar of his lion proclaimed him near,
    When Johnathan's eagle began to scream,
The fifer responded straightway to the call,
    And soon with his regiment, drilled therefor,
In spite of the enemy's powder and ball,
    Marched off to play in impending war.

Where strife was raging and hearts beat high,
    With dauntless courage that would not yield,
He helped to win, on the fifth of July,
    The bloody encounter on Chippewa's field.
Then chasing the foe to Niagara's shore,
    He there still mingled his patriot strain
With the booming of guns and the cataract's roar,
    At the subsequent battle of Lundy's Lane.

When war was over, the fifer returned,
    From fields of carnage and scenes of strife,
But still in his bosom there glowed and burned,
    A quenchless love for his martial fife.
As age drew on, it was still the same,
    He awaited the cars in his rustic seat,
And carrolled his welcome to all who came,
    Repeating his airs in the neighboring street.

On an empty box by the grocery store,
    He sat in the sun and piped away,
As if he imagined himself once more,
    Encouraging men to the deadly fray.

Or as if, perchance, in a milder mood,
   He wondered if ever grim war would cease,
Or whether his art would still be wooed,
   In the tranquil reign of the Prince of Peace.

When age and feebleness held him fast,
   Three days before the dread visitor came,
To bring him the summons which comes at last,
   He called for his fife; as the flickering flame
Flashed up once more; and his heart grew strong,
   His fingers resumed their cunning and skill,
The notes were clear he could not prolong,
   And now they are silent: his pulse is still.

The railroad vehicles come and go,
   The old sledge-hammer still sounds the wheels,
But Uncle Perry sleeps under the snow,
   And the heart instinctively, pensively feels
The force of the truth that 'tis all men's doom,
   That mortals approach to the farther shore;
The spring shall come, and the flowers shall bloom,
   But the merry old fifer may come no more.

CIV.

Tim stood a moment with a sober face,
   Which then resumed its humorous expression,
As he returned his "rostrum" to its place,
   And left the oratorical profession.
"Your girl can sing," he said, "with better grace,
   Than I can speak, and more of self possession;
And then we'll play at thimble-in-the-ring,
Or button, roll-the-plate, or some such thing;

CV.

"And when I kiss her in some kissing play,
   I may discover there was nothing in it;
Your prize may be a blank, you cannot say,
   If even it were possible to win it;

And all you know about her any way,
  Is what you learned in less than half a minute;
And she was kissing everybody then;
  Your 'magnetism' might have come from men,

CVI.

" Whose lips were pressing hers, for aught you know,
  And so have come to you but second-handed;
And if it should be proven that 'twas so,
  Your little skiff of love would then be stranded,
Like those you sailed about in long ago,
  Away up country, and yourself be landed
Among the breakers and the shoals once more,
Or high and dry upon the sandy shore."

CVII.

Will's laugh was half suggestive of a sigh,
  At least the humor seemed a little thin,
Although he laughed, and said, " I think I'll try
  Once more myself, as I've already been
Invited to repeat "—" The kiss? then why
  The dickens didn't you when you were in
A good position?" interrupted Tim;
But Will, resuming and correcting him,

CVIII.

Said, "No, the visit, my dear sir; you seem
  Somewhat facetious over this affair;
You may regard it as an idle dream,
  Or only as a castle in the air.
But, saying nothing of the kiss, I deem
  The lady interesting, who would bear
More intimate acquaintance; whom I may,
Or may not love; as yet I cannot say.

CIX.

"At all events she has invited me
  To come again, and ramble on the shore,
Along with her, and standing by the sea,
  And as we listen to its magic roar —"
"You'll ask her if she doesn't think 'twould be
  Agreeable to go to Rome once more,
And she one partner, you can be the other,
Unless she is attended by her mother,"

CX.

Said Tim, thus interrupting him again,
  And turning what he had begun to say,
From sentiment to humor; "like as when
  You found her trading in the store to-day,"
Continued he, "and if so, you'll be then,
  The same as now, compelled to come away,
The problem still unsolved." "And then," Will said,
"I'll go again; but now let's go to bed."

CXI.

And so they did, and so the case was rested,
  As we will rest anon, and Will returned
To where the scientific truths were tested,
  With which, at present, he was more concerned;
Although his heart was more or less congested,
  With its incipient love, which slowly burned,
The while his closing studies he pursued,
Or those of yore he hastily reviewed.

CXII.

He graduated shortly after that,
  And his diploma, written out in Latin —
A classic tongue, *ut gloriam efferat* —
  Contained the name — and named the chair he sat in —

Of him whose Breakfast Table Autocrat —
Although he hadn't then, I think, put that in
The public prints — has made him famed to-day,
For wit and wisdom, and " The One Hoss Shay."

CXIII.

And after graduation he began
To practice medicine, as doctors do —
But first we will discover, if we can,
If this new love affair of his, fell through,
Or if, for once, the course of true love ran
More smoothly than it is accustomed to —
But not until the canto is begun,
That is to say, the next succeeding one.

WILLOUGHBY'S WISDOM.

CANTO SIXTH.

I.

'Twas early summer; and the song of bird
    Fell on the grateful ear from wood and lea:
Glad nature's pulse had recently been stirred
    With new life vigor, like a soul set free;
But Nellie Ryder hadn't heard a word
    From Will, about his visit to the sea;
Although she knew the college course was done,
And of the graduates that he was one.

II.

She sat one day — one pleasant afternoon,
    Or early evening, in a rustic seat,
Upon the lawn; and, gazing at the moon,
    Whose growing disc was then almost complete,
Was singing pensively of bonnie Doon,
    Whose little warblers chanted notes so sweet,
Whose banks and braes could not have been more fair
Than field and lawn now blooming freshly there.

III.

While thus she sat, her father came along,
    From doing business at his grocery store,
And stopped to listen to the Scottish song,
    She half unconsciously was chiming o'er,

And laughing, said, "I hope there's nothing wrong
  With your 'false lover,' that you should deplore,
Unless it be that he has taken flight,
Where's that young doctor who was here the night

IV.

We had our gathering? I thought you said
  That he would come again another day:
He seemed a gentleman, at least well bred,
  I rather liked the fellow. By the way,
I have a letter for you which may shed
  Some light upon the subject; who can say?
I didn't know the hand, it may be his."
She opened it and, blushing, said, "It is."

V.

The father, whistling some familiar air,
  Went up the steps upon the portico,
And in the house, and left the daughter there;
  And she, with much of interest, I trow,
Was following the lines with anxious care,
  And what they were, the reader too shall know,
For thus she read, I thus transcribing it,
As hereinafter specified, to wit:

VI.

"Dear Madam — in the spring I promised you
  I'd call upon you later in the season,
And fear that I'm a little overdue,
  Although for that there's been sufficient reason;
And now I write the promise to renew,
  Lest I be guilty of a greater treason
To social obligation thus incurred,
To be fulfilled according to my word.

VII.

"And if, some night, which you will please to name,
 A hasty visit would be welcome still,
Or if preferred, some day would be the same,
 Some day or night, according to your will,
Or your convenience, I will own the claim
 Of pledge and promise, and will then fulfil;
And in return will call to your attention,
The ramble you were pleased to kindly mention;

VIII.

"Along the rugged edge, and up the steep
 Of Lynn's High Rock, or by the mystic sea;
To gaze upon 'the blue and moonlit deep,'
 From off the beach that you described to me;
A time and place to let the glamour creep
 O'er hearts that may be for the moment free
From toil and care, and from temptation too,
As free as watery deep or azure blue.

IX.

"And in our walks beneath the shining moon,
 We'll muse of nature's loveliness divine;
Or haply sit, through sunny afternoon,
 And calmly watch the peaceful day's decline;
And thank the Father for the precious boon
 Of joy that comes to your heart and to mine,
In contemplation of the moon's soft rays,
Or of the beauty of the summer days.

X.

"I trust you will excuse my long delay,
 And seeming negligence, for I have been
So much engaged I couldn't get away,
 With no excuse but visiting in Lynn;

But hope to see you at an early day,
    Expecting much of happiness therein,
Provided you express, in your reply,
    The wish that I should come: till then, good-by."

XI.

She read it through, and when the signature
    Had been pronounced, she looked it over still,
As if to make assurance doubly sure
    That 'twas a true expression of good will;
Not some hallucination to allure
    The heart into a hope foreboding ill;
For she, it may not be denied, was now
    More interested than she would avow.

XII.

Of course she wrote him in reply, although
    It may be deemed impertinent to tell
Just what she said; but as I chance to know,
    And as I think 'twould suit my readers well,
And as it is my duty to bestow
    On them the knowledge of just what befell,
I give the letter that she wrote, *verbatim*,
At *literatim*, even *punctuatim*.

XIII.

"Dear Sir — that I will welcome you almost
    At any time except when I'm in school,
I haste to tell you by return of post;
    And will suggest that when the moon is full,
'Tis more enchanting here upon the coast,
    Although a 'hasty visit,' as a rule,
Would be agreeable at any time,
And now especially in nature's prime.

XIV.

"As you request that I shall name the day,
    The 'day or night' which circumstances seem
To render most convenient, I will say
    That Friday of the present week I deem
The most available in every way,
    Of any one just now, and would esteem
It quite a privilege to see you then,
At four or five of post meridian.

XV.

"And you will make arrangements if you can,
    And if it be your pleasure, to remain,
At least till Saturday, that we may plan
    A visit to the beach, and to the chain
Of rocks behind the town, that I began
    To tell you of when here; but you will gain
A better knowledge than I gave you then,
When they are brought within the vision's ken.

XVI.

And in our wanderings, as you suggest,
    We'll muse upon the loveliness which here
Dame nature has so lavishly impressed
    On almost every object, far and near;
And for the joys with which our lives are blest,
    Be ever thankful, with a love sincere,
To Him who gave them; and that you may share
His blessings largely, is my wish and prayer."

XVII.

The letter finished and the name appended,
    She read it o'er to ascertain if she
Were free from errors, or they might be mended
    (A like experience occurs to me),

For in her words and sentences were blended
　　The hopes and fears of what was yet to be;
Which many a maiden's heart had felt before,
And doubtless will be felt by many more.

XVIII.

The coming Friday didn't fail to bring
　　The guest whom she had been so free to ask,
And to the door, in answer to his ring,
　　Soon after coming from her daily task
Of teaching school, she went, exhibiting
　　A pleasure which she didn't try to mask,
But frankly said, "I'm glad to see you sir;"
And no less cordially he greeted her.

XIX.

She led him through the hall, where coat and hat
　　Were hung upon the hat tree near the door,
That led into the parlor where they sat,
　　So many of them, several weeks before;
And now as then, she showed him into that,
　　But now no footsteps pressed upon the floor,
Save only theirs: no presence but their own;
And there for once, they found themselves alone.

XX.

And this was what he'd wanted ever since
　　They first had met, as we may well surmise,
But just the method which should best evince
　　His satisfaction, he could not devise.
I might, perhaps, have given him some hints,
　　Though I am not in such things over wise,
And then besides, it is my province now,
To tell you what he did, not tell him how.

XXI.

He tried to think of what he couldn't say
    The other time, for lack of opportunity;
But now the words had somehow slipped away,
    Just when he could have used them with impunity,
If not with good effect; and he — or they,
    Were both as silent as a staid community
Of Friends assembled, calmly waiting there,
To have the Spirit move to speech or prayer.

XXII.

'Twould not, however, do to so remain,
    And he could hardly frame his question whether
The time had dragged, or whether she would fain
    Have made it shorter ere they came together.
And she to think of something tried in vain,
    And therefore they resorted to the weather;
And one remarked the day was very fine,
Which answered well enough to the design

XXIII.

Of saying something, and 'twas very true,
    And Mrs. Ryder thereupon came in,
About the time this wise remark was through,
    And asking how he was and how he'd been,
Since he was there before, "I welcome you,"
    She said most pleasantly, "again to Lynn;"
Extending both her hands, the frequent mode
By which she welcomed friends to her abode.

XXIV.

As I have been received by some good dame,
    Of years and dignity, some dear old friend,
And one or two examples I could name,
    Of ladies who their greetings thus extend;

But then I might, perhaps, incur some blame —
    And broken friendship's rather hard to mend —
So I refrain from giving their address,
But leave it for my other friends to guess.

XXV.

And this time Will was glad to see the mother,
    For she had helped to dissipate the spell
Of awkwardness, which had, somehow or other,
    Crept in upon him, as it were the knell
Of self possession, all his wits to smother,
    Which ordinarily had served him well;
Which Mrs. Ryder thus restored him, when
Our youthful Richard was himself again.

XXVI.

At length they went the evening meal to get,
    When Mr. Ryder, coming from the store,
Gave Will a friendly greeting as they met,
    And chatted with him for an hour or more,
When they had eaten, till the sun had set,
    And he and Nellie started for the shore;
Which being rather out of easy reach,
Her father carried them upon the beach.

XXVII.

He said to Nellie, "Don't stay late, my dear,"
    And left them standing on the drifting sand.
The night was warm, the balmy atmosphere
    Was almost motionless on sea and land.
The stars were just beginning to appear,
    The moon ascending to the sky so grand,
It being full, while underneath it lay
A shining belt upon the watery way.

XXVIII.

Now Will and Nellie were alone once more,
    But circumstances had improved meanwhile,
And they could not but partially ignore
    Themselves, while looking out on sea and isle;
And what he had acquired of lovers' lore,
    Was more available; and lovers' guile,
He knew but little of in any hue,
Nor would he stoop to practice what he knew.

XXIX.

Yet I've no doubt he diligently tried
    To be agreeable, to please or charm;
He went around to the unusual side,
    And with his left hand gently clasped her arm;
And walking thus, looked forth upon the tide,
    Whose tiny, ceaseless waves could do no harm
To even such a web of gossamer
As he was weaving while he walked with her.

XXX.

He said "Miss Nellie," then he dropped the Miss,
    And called her simply by her given name;
Nor did she seem at all displeased at this,
    But grew familiar too, about the same,
In swift successive metamorphosis,
    As over both their hearts the "glamour" came,
The normal sequence of the "time and place,"
And all the circumstances of the case.

XXXI.

Thus long and sweetly did they walk and talk,
    The passing moments flying swiftly by,
Until their shadows gave them such a shock,
    On turning round to where they chanced to lie,

For they had grown so short; they seemed to mock
 Their joy, while pointing to the upper sky,
To which the moon had climbed, to such a height,
Approaching rapidly the noon of night.

XXXII.

"Oh dear!" said Nellie, "can it be so late,
 When Father said we mustn't stay? Oh dear!
Let's hurry homeward now at any rate,"
And taking out her watch, "why just look here,"
Continued she, "it's almost 'leven; fate
 Seems now against us, though I have no fear
Of being scolded, but I fear they may
Regard it wrong to thus have staid away."

XXXIII.

They hurried on as fast as they could go
 Conveniently, the moon still getting higher,
While they were coming down, as you must know,
 For rapid walking suffocates the fire
Then burning brightly in their breasts, although
 They still were harping on the golden lyre
Of, well, they hadn't called it love, 'tis true,
But friendship which for present use will do.

XXXIV.

Next day we find them basking in the sun,
 On famed High Rock, that overlooks the sea,
Nahant and Lynn between. The scene was one
 That, when I saw it, quite enchanted me.
The afternoon was scarcely yet begun,
 The sun declining in a slight degree,
And such a day we seldom look upon;
They come but rarely and they soon are gone.

XXXV.

I would describe it if I could, but no,
   'Twas one, of which, the summer season through,
Kind nature has but very few to show,
   And never in succession even two ;
So clear, so bright, so calm, so silent, so
   Extremely charming to admirers who
Are in accord with nature's harmonies,
And with the music of her melodies.

XXXVI.

They occupied a little grassy plot,
   With which the native rock was interspersed,
Which seemed to be a quite convenient spot,
   From which to look around; and they were versed
In that great art of seeing; and could not
   But be enamored of the scene at first,
But an enchantment of a different kind,
At length drove this one partly out of mind.

XXXVII.

They were as sociable as birds in spring;
   They seemed as fond as kitten, fawn or dove;
Though flung together as the fates will fling,
   They seemed to fit each other like a glove.
They freely talked of almost everything,
   Of friendship and, though sparingly, of love,
Whereon they both appeared to be intent,
But as to which they both were reticent.

XXXVIII.

But by and by he looked in Nellie's eyes,
   A little pensively, while in his own
He felt the moisture, though he could disguise
   Its presence for a time, till it had grown

Somewhat persistent, when with some surprise,
    At such a weakness, which had thus been shown,
He quickly brushed the starting tear away,
    And earnestly proceeded thus to say:

XXXIX.

" 'Tis but a day, and scarcely yet a day —
    The hours have told but twenty since I came;
And they so rapidly have slipped away,
    That if 'twere one 'twould seem almost the same;
And but for one thing I could truly say —
    And that is one for which I take some blame,
And doubtless you will blame me more or less —
I should have been in constant happiness.

XL.

" And now I must apologize to you,
    If I have wronged you, as I really fear
I may have done to some extent, in view
    Of certain facts which I must tell you here;
Because to simple justice it is due,
    As well as friendship, if it be sincere,
As ours appears to be, and as I fain
Would know that it forever might remain.

XLI.

" 'Twould be presumptuous, should I assume
    That you were waiting for a proposition,
And thereupon endeavor to illume
    Your mind in reference to the condition
Of my affairs; and yet I may presume
    That you at least will grant me your permission,
To say that, were it not for honor's due,
I should present my heart and hand to you.

XLII.

"But many years ago I loved another;
    A boyish love, and one I sought to shun;
Thus being counselled by an older brother,
    'Don't get in love before you're twenty-one;'
And thinking he was right, I tried to smother
    The passion, which I partially had done;
But this new love revives the old. Somehow,
I cannot drive her image from me now.

XLIII.

"It happened so that I had rendered her
    A trifling service, and her gratitude
Made quite a hero of me, as it were,
    And made me think that I should not intrude,
By calling on her; that I should confer
    A favor rather, so I oft renewed
My visits for a little while, and she,
Apparently, grew rather fond of me,

XLIV.

"As well as I of her; although I said,
    Not half as much as I have said to you,
In fact said nothing of my love, instead
    Of which, I simply promised to be true
To friendship, as we called it, though it led
    To something more on my part; but in view
Of what I meant to do, I tried to quell
My love, and so I lost my friend as well.

XLV.

"I'd known her but a fortnight, more or less —
    Perhaps three weeks — before I left the place;
And through my resolution to suppress
    My strong attachment — though to my disgrace —

I didn't write her for a year, I guess,
   And now I doubt if I should know her face:
And when I did write, she made no reply,
But I have never known the reason why."

XLVI.

"And you propose," said Nellie, with a sigh,
   "When you get back, to look her up again;"
And he could see the moisture in her eye,
   And thought she hadn't looked so sweet as then; —
"And then," said she, "you may discover why
   She didn't write to you in answer, when
You'd written her. Well, Heaven bless you, Will,
And if you marry her, God bless you still."

XLVII.

He pressed her hand and said, "'Twill not be so,
   I think; at least 'tis not what I expect;
She wasn't quite sixteen — eight years ago —
   And her development and my neglect,
Have left small room for such a love to grow,
   And she would now be likely to reject
My suit, and yet it might be wrong to " — here
He stopped, and on her hand there fell a tear.

XLVIII.

O love of woman! passion hard to smother,
   In any age or section of the globe;
O woman! who, as sister, wife or mother,
   Art fitly decked with angel's crown and robe;
O women! who are hateful to each other,
   As ever Satan was to righteous Job;
Both saint and sinner worship at thy shrine,
And deem thou art half human, half divine.

XLIX.

The reader may object that 'tisn't fair,
    To get the boy in love with everybody,
And may insist that no true love was there,
    But that 'twas only sentimental shoddy;
And in a general way we may declare
    That every boy that falls in love's a noddy,
Except my hero when he chanced to fall so,
Of course excepting my young readers also.

L.

But Will had never loved but two or three,
    And I had loved as many most sincerely,
Before I ever was as old as he,
    When he went down to Lynn; and he was clearly
In love with two at once in some degree; —
    I've known a man to marry almost yearly,
The sorrows and the ills of life to soften,
And sometimes they have " done it once too often:"

LI.

As did the senior Weller, as he said
    To Sammy, when he cautioned him to shun
" The vidders," and in fact, whoe'er would wed
    The senior Weller's interesting son.
You recollect how circumstances led
    To quite a boyish fancy for the one
Will learned to dance with, whom, to some extent,
He early loved, but who, as matters went,

LII.

Refusing first a young collegiate,
    On whom her heart its love would not confer,
Long ere 'twas time that he should choose a mate,
    Had wed a worthy youth who courted her,

And Will surrendered to an adverse fate,
  In that particular, if such it were,
But never lost the old respect he had
For her, a lass, when he was but a lad.

LIII.

So there was no great reason to regret
  The termination of his first affair,
Of but incipient love, but when he met
  With Nellie, it was time he should beware;
For he by no means had forgotten yet,
  The girl at Mrs. Grant's, and couldn't bear
The thought of what he otherwise would do,
Until he knew if she remembered too.

LIV.

Nor could he think of leaving Nellie so,
  To go in search of one he hadn't seen,
Or heard from, since so many years ago;
  And like St. Paul, was in a strait between
The two attractions; for he didn't know
  Which way to turn him, or which way to lean,
While love's divided stream was coursing through him,
When Nellie made a proposition to him.

LV.

"I'm sure," she said, "that I've no claim on you,
  Against this prior one; you first shall see
If she the old attachment would renew;
  And if so, well; if not, come back to me.
And yet all this requires a short adieu,
  My long lost, dear old friend, for I am she."
And thus revealing what she long had kept,
She fondly fell upon his neck and wept.

LVI.

The language of a tear! in grief or joy,
   'Tis most expressive of the heart's emotions;
Although 'tis said some people can employ
   Their tears as stock in trade; like Yankee notions;
And some good honest heart thereby decoy,
   By false pretenses, into true devotions;
Yet I regard it in its native fitness,
In almost every case, an honest witness.

LVII.

But those of Will and Nellie soon were dry,
   And they were living over "auld lang syne,"
And looking forward to the by and by,
   Around which all our hearts their hopes entwine;
And they could now look on the deep blue sky,
   And "calmly watch the peaceful day's decline;"
And when it had declined, they too descended,
And joyfully their homeward way they wended.

LVIII.

They reached the house in time for supper, when
   She quickly ushered in her old gallant,
And said, "O mother, he's the same as then,
   O Will, don't you remember Mrs. Grant?
If not, I'll introduce to you again,
   My dearest life-long friend, my former aunt,
With whom I lived when first we knew each other,
And she soon afterwards became my mother."

LIX.

'Twill be remembered that the gossippers,
   Who intermeddle so in our affairs,
Made no exception in regard to hers;—
   They often have us married unawares:

It is a favor which the world confers
　　On "single blessedness;" and never cares
For truth, though she, as they had not belied her,
Had subsequently married Julius Ryder.

LX.

She was an aunt, though not by consanguinity,
　　To Nellie, and 'twas on her mother's side,
Her mother's brother's wife, thus by affinity
　　Related to them only; so she tried
This new relationship, as 'twere a trinity
　　Of mother, wife and aunt; and none denied
That she had filled the three positions well,
And all the joys of home had helped to swell.

LXI.

Step-mothers oftentimes are humbugs; so
　　Are second husbands' children none the less,
As many a hapless child has come to know,
　　And many a woman who had sought to bless
Some motherless young brood. The embers glow,
　　On altars of domestic happiness,
But feebly oft, though that we cannot say,
Of Mrs. Ryder and her protégée.

LXII.

The marriage had occurred in early spring,
　　Succeeding their so short acquaintanceship
With Will; but neither told him anything
　　Of that, perhaps as the proverbial slip,
That chance and adverse circumstance may bring
　　Between the cup and the expectant lip,
Had made them reticent concerning it,
As prudent dames have often deemed most fit.

LXIII.

And when the marriage rites had taken place,
    They had no tidings from the truant boy;
Nor had they any means by which to trace
    His journeyings; and therefore Helen's joy
Was incomplete: her father's fond embrace
    Conveyed a pleasure not without alloy; —
Nor did she ever get the letter Will
Had written her, or hear from him until

LXIV.

They introduced her to him in the hall
    At Dr. Hathaway's, as said before;
And she had then abandoned nearly all
    Her hopes of ever hearing from him more.
His looks contained but little she could call
    To mind, and she resolved that she'd ignore
The old acquaintance now, and would remain
Incognito to him, and ascertain,

LXV.

If possible, the reason why he should
    Have thus deserted her in former days;
And that she would recover, if she could,
    His friendship at the least, in other ways
Than by demanding it; and failing, would
    Conceal her former self still from his gaze.
She sought new love, the old meanwhile to screen,
With what result, we've now already seen.

LXVI.

They named her Helen Mabel, at her birth,
    The former being given for her aunt;
But when her mother passed away from earth,
    Or when she went to live with Mrs. Grant,

The latter called her Mabel, for its worth,
 But more for its convenience; to supplant
The name of Helen, as it was her own,
Still used by some old friends she long had known.

LXVII.

But on returning to her native place,
 Where all had known so well the name she bore,
That being as familiar as her face,
 It then was Helen, as in days of yore;
But an improvement having come to grace
 This sweet old name, some little time before,
They called her Nellie; to distinguish her
From this new mother, as I now infer.

LXVIII.

I said the story that I had in mind,
 Would not be one of love; but it has carried
Much more of that than I at first designed;
 Before its altar I too long have tarried.
And now the reader will be glad to find
 That Will and Nellie presently were married;
And settled down to the domestic bliss,
That comes of marriage in a world like this.

LXIX.

Thus many a wooing has turned out since Eve's,
 'Tis native fruit and men are prone to pluck it;
They fall in love as fall the autumn leaves;
 They seek for happiness, and think they've struck it;
And maidens reason as did Mrs. Reeves,
 Whose home was in the island of Nantucket;
Wherein she used to keep an old museum
Of curiosities, and let you see 'em,

LXX.

For due consideration. She was bred
 A Quakeress, and when a young man came
To ask her hand, whose soul had not been fed
 On Quaker diet, she was held to blame,
That she did not reject him; but she said,
 To those opposing her, " Pray can you name
Some Quaker youth of whom I may be sure,
If I this gentile suitor should abjure ? "

LXXI.

I like the Quakers, and I loved the fair,
 Though aged lady of that island town,
Who was so kind to me when I was there,
 And who in queenly fashion wore the crown
Of noble womanhood. I hardly dare
 To give her name, lest I incur the frown
Of one whose memory delights me now,
As when I listened to her thee and thou.

LXXII.

I called upon her first to thus renew
 The old acquaintance of a teacher, when
My own accomplishments were very few;
 And she invited me to call again,
Which I was very glad to do, in view
 Of her intelligence concerning men
And things, whereof she talked without restraint,
As also of Nantucket, old and quaint;

LXXIII.

And once so prosperous — in days of yore —
 When every ocean recognized her sail,
When she pursued her prey the wide world o'er,
 Subsisting, as did Jonah, on the whale.

But she, like him, at length was cast ashore,
   When gas and kerosene began to pale
Her feeble light, and so restrict her gains,
But much of her old quaintness still remains.

LXXIV.

The promenades that frequently adorn
   The roofs of houses — with their shingled sides —
Wherefrom old residents, at night or morn,
   Could see what ships were floating on the tides:
The village crier, with his bell and horn,
   Still stalks about the streets with rapid strides,
Proclaiming to the world, with much ado,
What has occurred or is expected to.

LXXV.

They sell their meat upon the auction block,
   The crier heralding their beef and ham; —
"There'll be a meat-ox, half past ten o'clock,
   At Burgess' market, corned beef, mutton, lamb,
At half past ten o'clock, meat-ox." Their stock,
   Their local history says — to which I am
Indebted for the record of a case —
They thus dispose of in the market-place.

LXXVI.

Although Nantucket has released her hold
   Upon the whale, and he her holds deserted,
She has, as I, when I was there, was told,
   And as 'twas very commonly asserted,
Like Peter and the fishermen of old,
   When they to Christian faith had been converted,
To some extent at least, "struck oil" again,
Her people being fishers now " of men."

LXXVII.

That is to say, they've learned to advertise
    The island as a " favorite resort,"
For summer tourists, whom I may advise
    That 'tis a pleasant place to make a short
Sojourn upon; nor would it be unwise,
    In those who have sufficient leisure for't,
To make a longer stay; at least to me,
It seemed a gem in the surrounding sea.

LXXVIII.

And there Will planned to take his bridal tour;
    And would have done so, as I chance to know,
But that he had as yet been kept so poor,
    'Twas rather inconvenient then to go,
To any distance, though I'm pretty sure
    They took a sail to Hull or Hingham, so
As not to altogether lose the trip,
That should begin a marriage partnership.

LXXIX.

And later in the season, he returned,
    To father, mother and his native place:
The time for which his heart so long had yearned,
    At length had come to him by Heaven's grace.
Through all the years, within his bosom burned,
    A love of home that time could not efface,
Until he had, among its olden charms,
Been fondly folded in his mother's arms.

LXXX.

His brother George was married — settled down,
    And fairly prosperous upon a farm,
Half way between his father's and the town;
    His home already had the added charm

Of two small feet beneath a baby gown; —
   His younger sister seemed to see no harm,
Almost while she was still embracing him,
In asking rather fondly after Tim.

LXXXI.

They welcomed Nellie in a kindly way,
   Though Mr. Hayden had been prejudiced
Against her slightly ever since the day
   Will first had written them of her, the gist
Of which, through preconceived opinions, lay
   In that she was an educationist,
As he adhered to his old notion still,
That knowledge necessarily was ill,

LXXXII.

For common people; it belonged to those
   Who somehow had been fortunately born
Thereto; and this young lady, when she chose
   To marry Will, was of her birthright shorn,
If e'er she had it. He could not suppose
   The flimsy vail so easy to be torn,
Between plebeians and patricians, who
May change positions, as they often do.

LXXXIII.

And Will, as rated by his father, seemed
   A sort of "upstart," who had left the sphere
That he belonged in; whose success he deemed
   Almost impossible; and it was clear
That if his merits should be thus esteemed,
   By everybody, that would interfere
With his prosperity, but still he thought
The world at large would rate him as it ought.

LXXXIV.

He hesitated some concerning whether
   'Twere best to settle in his native town,
Or better to abandon altogether,
   His home and birthplace, and again go down
And settle by the sea; but stress of weather,
   Wherein his father found himself — a frown
Of fickle fortune — answered for him, as
Some unforeseen occurrence often has.

LXXXV.

Existence any way is perilous,
   And Mr. Hayden found, one fateful day,
That his, just then especially, was thus,
   When, turning round, his horse had got away;
A dislocation of the humerus,
   As with the scapula, that is to say,
A dislocated shoulder being what
Resulted from it. Will, however, thought

LXXXVI.

'Twould not be difficult to then reduce
   The dislocation, as he soon suggested;
But here his father interposed a truce,
   And said he'd wait, he being interested;
Nor did he deign to offer an excuse
   For nonconsent to have the matter tested;
But simply said, "You go and get a doctor."
O Harvard! Harvard! how it would have shocked her.

LXXXVII.

And Will was rather nonplussed, I suspect,
   At such an order, yet did not demur;
Nor did he his allotted task neglect,
   But went and got the mare and started her

Directly for the town. He little recked
  What pre-existing notions of him were,
But thinking over what he hoped to do,
He said, "I'll show him I'm a doctor too."

LXXXVIII.

He overtook at length, upon the road,
  Old Dr. Whitman, whom they had employed
Aforetime; and he noticed that he showed
  The marks of age, and what he had enjoyed,
That he was slowly nearing the abode
  Where happiness, they say, is unalloyed.
He did his errand and they turned about,
And both went back to help the father out.

LXXXIX.

His arm was swollen more than at the first,
  More difficult to set in consequence,
Though Dr. Whitman said 'twas not the worst
  That might have come to him. "A little hence,"
Continued he, "if this young man is versed
  In such affairs, we will at least commence
The operation;" and they soon succeeded,
Will rendering assistance when 'twas needed.

XC.

Two doctors practised at the village then,
  One being old and rich: the other one
Had ridden several years, some eight or ten,
  And it was evident that he'd begun
To take the lead from Dr. Whitman, when
  The latter met with Will. And when he'd done
For Mr. Hayden what he could, he said
To Will, while sitting by his father's bed,

XCI.

" Where had you thought of hanging out your shingle?
    I'm half inclined to want to keep you here;
For five and forty years I've practised single,
    But I grow lazy now from year to year;
I never fancied very much the jingle
    Of doctors' partnerships, but you appear
Quite well informed, perhaps you'd like to try
The thing a while together, you and I.

XCII.

" I'd like to set you on your feet; besides,
    I'd like to knock my rival off his pins."
A sweet benevolence, which thus divides,
    In generous fashion, with the common sins
Of selfishness and envy. Conscience strides
    Into the saddle when the race begins,
But leaves one stirrup empty all the while,
For such companionship as may beguile

XCIII.

The dull monotony of virtue's ways.
    " The apparatus I've already got,
Some horses, books, a practice still that pays,"
    He said, " and might have more as well as not,
If I could do as in the early days
    I did do, when I showed them what was what,
As you can now if you will do the work
That I did then, which now I'd like to shirk."

XCIV.

The conversation then grew scientific,
    Or rather technical, as also quizzical;
As Dr. Whitman seemed to be prolific
    Of questions appertaining to the physical

Of man ; and what was reckoned a specific,
   For his diseases, dropsical or phthisical,
Acute or chronic ; much of which was said,
   To ascertain if Will were fairly read.

XCV.

While they conversed, and Mr. Hayden lay,
   A silent listener, their words, somehow,
Began to drive the cloud of mist away,
   Through which he'd looked at both of them till now ;
Until the doctor seemed but common clay,
   And Will was competent, he must allow,
To talk intelligently, and sustain
His own position in fair science' fane.

XCVI.

And then the glamour of distinction seemed,
   To Mr. Hayden, to be growing less.
Approaching deities are less esteemed
   Than those who dwell in some far off recess :
The ancient gods of wood and stone were deemed
   But representatives of mightiness —
Of gods who ruled the destinies of man,
From far away, as Jupiter or Pan.

XCVII.

" No man's a hero to his valet," so
   An old French writer said, and so I view it.
No set of men are heroes whom we know,
   No calling sacred to those who pursue it.
Its halo loses largely of the glow,
   With which it was surrounded ere they knew it,
Except by vague and magnified impressions,
As Mr. Hayden did the learned professions.

XCVIII.

When, by his deeds of love and virtue done,
    Had Jesus, long ago, made such a stir,
They asked each other, " Isn't this the son
    Of Joseph (whom they knew) the carpenter?"
" Can any good thing," grimly queried one;
    "Come out of Nazareth?" as if it were
Not fit that any mighty things should be
Accomplished by a son of Galilee.

XCIX.

Thus Mr. Hayden had regarded Will,
    As natively inferior to those
He thought were born to higher life, until
    He saw them face to face, and saw him pose
So well with one who used to have, and still
    Had many a healing balm for human woes;
But when the other left with words like these,
" You'll pay the junior partner if you please,"

C.

He would have trusted him to even set
    A dislocated shoulder, though 'tis wise,
I think myself, to let young doctors get
    Their practice slowly, and to exercise
Their talents under supervision yet
    A little while, until they've learned to prize
Experience, as well as education, which
It is her province largely to enrich.

CI.

Will went to town to prearrange details,
    The Dr. offered him some rooms up stairs,
And partly furnished, from the fair avails
    Of his prosperity. Some slight repairs,

Or changes, prompted him to say, " What ails
   It now for keeping house?" and their affairs
Appeared to him and Nellie both to be
Quite promising, so far as they could see.

CII.

He waited patiently and patientless,
   Except his father, for a week or two,
And that, though not the very best success,
   Was not the worst that young physicians do;
A hasty call, a patient in distress,
   The case unlike the ones presented through
The books and lectures, as they seemed to be,
Has puzzled many a newly fledged M. D.

CIII.

But by and by his senior had a call,
   To go and see a man who, gruff and grim,
Lived on the mountain slope; whose turbid gall
   Had made him feel, that day, "uncommon slim."
The evening shadows had begun to fall,
   And so the Dr. sent Will up to him.
When he arrived, he found the man in bed,
In spite of which, he vigorously said,

CIV.

" I sent for Dr. Whitman, whom I knew,
   Before you ever saw the light of day;
When I want you to come, I'll send for you,
   And that is all, young man, I have to say."
And Will concluded it were best, in view
   Of what he had said, that he come away;
But Dr. Whitman laughed and said, " We'll find
Another for you shortly, never mind."

CV.

And sure enough, next day, when he was gone,
   To see the one who thus rejected Will,
A young man came who said they sent him on,
   To get a doctor for some children, ill
With scarlatina; and he went anon,
   And this time managed so to fill the bill,
As to commence a practice which increased
As fast as he expected, at the least.

CVI.

Nate Alden's wife — and we will not go back
   To where we last saw Nate, except to say
That he, alas! pursued the downward track,
   That gaming took the place of harmless play,
And drink came also in its wake, to sack
   The moral citadel, and take away
Still more of virtue, righteousness and truth,
The priceless jewels of both age and youth.

CVII.

His wife, whom Will had slightly known of yore,
   Came early to him to implore his aid;
To know if, through his Esculapian lore,
   Some new discovery had not been made —
Or if some remedy were known before —
   By which the ghost of Bacchus could be laid;
And then perchance his gambling habit might
Be broken up, and he be set aright.

CVIII.

Will said the ailment was a moral one,
   Which only moral remedies would touch;
And in the present case so long had run,
   That even they might not accomplish much;

But if the treatment were to be begun,
  The circumstances of the case were such
As might suggest, he thought, as being fit,
Some method like the following, to wit:

CIX.

He said, "If I were you, I'd try instanter,
  The homœpathic system, which is this,
'*Similia, similibus, curantur,*'
  Or 'like cures like,' which might not come amiss:
And you, perhaps, could be the wise enchanter,
  To conjure up the metamorphosis,
From guilt to innocence, without the loss
Of gold or crucible, or even dross.

CX.

"That is, if pleasure's dross, as we are told,
  By those who would persuade us to eschew it,
Although the contrary is true, I hold;—
  According to the light in which I view it,
All righteous pleasures are but sands of gold,
  When life is waning, helping to renew it;
But Nathan simply carries things too far,
And tries to get more pleasures than there are.

CXI.

"And now, if anything, I would propose
  That you yourself, at once begin to play
At euchre, high-low-jack, and games like those;
  And thus induce him, if you can, to stay
Much more at home. The places where he goes,
  Are bad; and if he could be kept away,
His vices might, perhaps, be overgrown,
By something better, heretofore unknown."

CXII.

But Mrs. Alden sadly shook her head,
    As if it were a point she couldn't see;
She didn't hold to playing cards, she said,
    And then the deacon and his wife would be
So shocked, and deem that she was so ill bred —
    They lived at Deacon Alden's, Nate and she,
And so were hedged about by virtues such
As gain so little while they seek so much.

CXIII.

When Rev. Mr. Talmage says, " I hail
    The rod of fisherman and sportsman's gun "—
Those cruel implements — why should he quail
    Before the ace of spades, or turn and run,
From euchre more than chess? Why should he fail
    To recognize the little boyish fun
That comes of seven-up, old sledge or whist,
And put them on his recreation list?

CXIV.

Nate would have furnished rather poor material,
    With which to try a nice experiment,
And such experiments must needs be serial,
    To show if they would be beneficent:
Will's moral castle might have proved aerial,
    Or more substantial but by accident;
But as he couldn't try his method so,
We cannot say if it were wise or no.

CXV.

Will thence proceeded on his peaceful way,
    And helped his fellows when and where he could,
And helped himself, it is but fair to say,
    As others do, and as perhaps they should;

We all to some extent are beasts of prey,
　And he was but comparatively good,
And as the story is so nearly through,
　We'll only follow him a year or two.

CXVI.

The lamps were lighted in the quiet town,
　Where he and Nellie lived; and Nellie rose
From where she sat, and laid the baby down,
　He having now forgotten all his woes,
When Dr. Whitman's wife, whose locks of brown
　Were being whitened by the falling snows
Of age, came up the stairs to ask if she
Would meet the ladies of the church, to see

CXVII.

About the coming yearly festival,
　And make arrangements for it, such as would
Be best adapted to the annual
　Associations of the brotherhood,
In social gathering; the prodigal
　To be invited with the "unco good,"
And asked to spend his substance there in giving,
If not in riotous and rapid living.

CXVIII.

The meeting was at Mrs. Whitman's, so
　'Twould not be very inconvenient then,
For Nellie, while the baby slept, to go;
　And Will would probably be back again,
From visiting some village patients; though
　He didn't come till rather late, and when
He did, they asked him to the council too,
To hear of what they had designed to do.

CXIX.

And say if their designs should yet be changed,
  For they had got them pretty well laid out,
Though one or two were partially estranged
  From what was general, and were in doubt
As to the wisdom of the plans arranged,
  Which they were still in some debate about;
Although the great majority were still
In favor of them, when they called on Will.

CXX.

The proposition was to introduce
  Some lottery schemes, by which to sell some things
They'd bought and made, for ornament or use,
  At higher prices than the market brings;
For which they merely offered the excuse,
  That 'twas for righteousness, which often flings
Its mantle over doubtful methods, such
As common sinners cannot safely touch.

CXXI.

They'd had the same thing once or twice before —
  Substantially the same — and liked it well;
At least they liked the golden fruit it bore,
  It having helped materially to swell
The gross amount of what they had in store; —
  'Twas a commodity that seemed to sell:
Hence they proposed on this occasion, when
The time should come, to offer it again.

CXXII.

"What says the Dr.?" asked a lady who
  Had engineered it largely, whereupon
Will rose and said, "'Tis not my province to
  Attempt to dictate, either pro or con;

But I will tell you what I tried to do,
   An hour ago or so, while I was gone,
As yet apparently without success,
But I consistently could do no less.

CXXIII.

" I had a patient at the tavern, whom
   I went to see a little after dark,
And in the hall, when coming from his room,
   I met three fellows who were on a lark.
The light was rather dim, but in the gloom,
   I saw their faces, and I knew Bert Clark,
And Nathan Alden, Deacon Alden's son,
But didn't recollect the other one.

CXXIV.

" 'Say Doc,' ejaculated Nate, ' come in,
   Along with us; perhaps you'd like to play
A game of poker — either lose or win,
   And I've done more or less of both to-day.'
And as they were about to re-begin,
   I went into the room where he and they
Were playing ' penny poker;' or at least
They had been, but at supper time had ceased.

CXXV.

" They all sat down, and left a place for me,
   Requesting me to take it. ' No,' said I,
' I incidentally dropped in to see
   What you were doing, and to also try
To get you all to promise and agree
   To neither drink nor gamble.' Nate's reply
Was singularly pertinent, I thought,
To one of the proposals I had brought.

CXXVI.

"'No doubt,' he said, 'it is a pleasant thing
    To be so virtuous and good and true;'
Then holding up his hand so as to bring
    His little finger into plainer view,
Continued, 'do you know I got that ring,
    By gambling for it in the church that you
Belong to now, of which my father was
The senior deacon? Better have a clause

CXXVII.

Inserted in the creed or government,
    That shall prevent the wicked practice there;
And then its emissaries may be sent
    To places where they gamble fair and square,
With some consistency.' Bert said, 'I spent
    What money at the church I had to spare,
But I had nothing for it when I'd done.
The chances here are better, two to one.'

CXXVIII.

"I made reply by saying what I could,
    And say it honestly, in such a case,
But that was little, and that Nathan should
    Have made his statement with so good a grace,
And that I knew that he could make it good,
    And at his pleasure throw it in my face,
I much regretted; and I could but see,
That he in some sense had the best of me.

CXXIX.

"And now you may, perhaps, anticipate,
    What, speaking further, I would further say;
But I intended simply to relate
    What came to me in this peculiar way;

And you the lesson may appropriate,
  Or may reject its teaching, yea or nay :
'Tis not my province, as I said before,
To dictate to you, and I'll say no more."

CXXX.

This tale is one of fiction ; or in part
  Fictitious, though with much of truth combined ;
But true, according to the mystic art
  Of story telling — or at least designed
To be so — to the facts of history's chart ;
  Or true to nature, as in humankind
Developed ; but I'm not prepared to show
If their designs were carried out or no.

CXXXI.

I've preached that way myself from year to year,
  And now church lotteries are less in fashion ;
But whether from the preaching, isn't clear,
  Or whether from subsidence of the passion ;
The clearing of the moral atmosphere,
  The enterprising and devout Caucasian
Has been surrounded by ; the world's advance
In knowledge, which all virtues should enhance.

CXXXII.

" Kind nature gives our blood a moral flow,"
  Somebody says, from whom my memory quotes,
And this of churches, as of men, is so,
  Although their eyes contain some moral motes,
Which seems to make their progress rather slow,
  Though just as sure — from all prophetic notes —
As e'er my hero's was, when nature gave him,
Of moral leanings, just enough to save him.

CXXXIII.

And if she's done as much for you and me,
   And given us the aspirations high,
That tend to make us what we ought to be,
   And lead us gently to the by and by
Of truth and righteousness — for all so free —
   We should be thankful for it, you and I,
And ever pray that we may thus be led,
Till all our sins are crucified and dead.

CXXXIV.

My story's told. It was designed to show
   What may be done by culture and progression.
I took an ordinary boy, you know,
   And one who, at the time, was in possession
Of ordinary faculties; which grow
   By normal use; and in the learned profession,
Which he had chosen for a livelihood,
He sought his own and others' highest good.

CXXXV.

And in the same direction both must lie —
   No man may wrong his fellows with impunity,
And whoso would be blest himself, must try
   To bless mankind, as he has opportunity;
And much of happiness will come thereby;
   Because men's interests are more in unity,
Than in the selfish past they e'er have seemed;
Than kings and conquerors have ever dreamed.

CXXXVI.

Life is at best a game, and he who plays
   By nature's honest rules, is sure to win;
Although at times, in this world's crooked ways,
   His tricks are taken by the trumps of sin:

But he a broad and deep foundation lays,
    And when at length the cards are gathered in —
When all dissimulation shall have ceased —
He'll surely have the odd one at the least.

CXXXVII.

The sweets of life should sparingly be tasted,
    Or haply left untasted as we pass.
With selfish pleasures life is often wasted,
    And we are left to cry, alas! alas!
And nature has her placards duly pasted
    On post and fence and tree, "Keep off the grass,"
As city fathers do on boulevards; —
And none may safely scale the moral bars.

CXXXVIII.

The good alone are happy. Even they
    Are so entangled in the sin and woe
Of those behind them in the upward way,
    That unmixed happiness they seldom know.
And yet that vice was never made to "pay,"
    As virtue does, the facts of life will show,
Should they be traced sufficiently to see
What their legitimate results may be.

CXXXIX.

The moral world, so little understood,
    Is one of justice and of recompense,
Wherein alone the evil and the good
    Are both determined by the inner sense
Of well developed man and womanhood
    Of noble aspirations, gleaning thence
Some slight capacity to rightly read
The higher law and the diviner creed.

CXL.

To build a character, and do it well,
 Should be the aim of life; and yet how few,
In moral architecture so excel,
 As even Willoughby; who might review
His life with some regrets, for what befell
 Therein of wrong and error, which may you,
My reader, shun, at least in some degree,
Acquiring more of wisdom than did he.

www.ingramcontent.com/pod-product-compliance
Lightning Source LLC
Chambersburg PA
CBHW031744230426
43669CB00007B/469